NO MORE DAMNED SECRETS

NO MORE DAMNED SECRETS

An Anglo-Canadian War Child's Quest
for Roots and Identity

To Elizabeth Buchanan

Paul Cornes

With warmest wishes,

Paul Cornes.

14 April 2013

Book Guild Publishing

Sussex, England

First published in Great Britain in 2013 by
The Book Guild Ltd
Pavilion View
19 New Road
Brighton, BN1 1UF

Typesetting in Garamond by
YHT Ltd, London

Printed and bound in Great Britain by
CPI Group (UK) Ltd, Croydon, CR0 4YY

A catalogue record for this book is available from
The British Library.

ISBN 978 1 84624 825 2

For Fay

From voyages of discovery
to distant lands of ancestry,
I am your sailor, home from sea.

Contents

Introduction

During the Second World War, a half-million Canadian servicemen were stationed in the United Kingdom. Some met and married British women, the war brides who, with their children, joined them in Canada after the war. Other relationships, ranging from casual encounters to more serious, but ultimately broken romances, had less happy endings. In addition to a trail of abortions, the Canadians left behind around 22,000 illegitimate children. The more fortunate were raised by their mothers – sometimes as lone parents, sometimes in partnership with men they later married, or grandparents, as was the case for Eric Clapton. The less fortunate were placed for adoption or spent their childhood in institutional care. Like the subjects of Margaret Humphreys' *Empty Cradles*, some may even have been shipped overseas as child migrants.

Those 'war children' are now in their late sixties and early seventies, generally living in retirement with children and grandchildren of their own. Many, including some who only quite late in life have discovered the circumstances in which they were conceived, have nurtured a desire to make contact with their fathers or, most probably now, paternal kith and kin. But the Canadian government has steadfastly declined to accept any responsibility for its war children or offer effective help with their searches. Moreover, official denial appears to have been aided and abetted by Canada's politicians and historians, who have done very little to acknowledge this neglected aspect of their country's wartime history.

The 'cover-up' was so effective that, as recently as 2005, after hearing evidence about the war children at a meeting of the

1

Parliamentary Standing Committee on Citizenship and Immigration, Andrew Telegdi, a distinguished Canadian politician and long serving member and chair of that committee, stated that he found it 'incredibly disturbing' that information about those war children had not previously been presented to the committee and that Canada appeared to have washed its hands of the matter.

The reader will find in these pages an account of the discovery, after my mother's death in 2001, that I was one of those war children and how my initial response to that information was to bury it – to let matters lie. I took the view that there was little to be gained from dwelling on the past. History could not be re-written. Also, I was quite apprehensive about what might be revealed if I started to turn over those stones. But that attempt at studied indifference didn't work. The outrage experienced when first informed about my origins did not dissipate. Rather, it became associated with the build-up of a volatile magma chamber of emotion, which on two or three occasions surfaced in the form of sudden, embarrassingly tearful and angry eruptions.

Evidently, the past refused to be buried. So it was, following the last of those episodes around four years after my mother's demise, I decided upon a different, hopefully more cathartic tack, and set myself the task of tracing my Canadian father, about whom the only information I had was a name. The aim was to provide myself and my children and grandchildren with a more authentic account of our shared family history than had been disclosed hitherto.

Pursuit of that objective proved to be an emotional roller-coaster ride with many surprises; some pleasant, others not so. The least pleasant was the disclosure of a deliberately spun, multi-layered web of deceit. It had been woven by my mother with the complicity of her sisters and other family members and was intended to prevent me from ever finding out about the events and circumstances that led to my birth. She had sworn them to an oath of secrecy, a family *omertà*, to which they considered themselves bound long after she passed away. Consequently, the earlier stages of my enquiries were undertaken with at best minimal assistance from that quarter and, to this day, I am not confident the co-conspirators told me all that there was to tell. In any event, as will be revealed, at the time they had good reason to maintain their silence.

Their resistance persuaded me to re-visit my childhood and adolescence. That retrospective 'journey' helped to shed light on numerous incidents and interactions, the meaning of which had previously been either difficult to comprehend or, in some instances, simply inexplicable. It certainly offered some explanation for the sense of difference and the absence of a strong feeling of belonging that I experienced during those formative years. In turn, that led to questions about the extent to which the family dynamics underlying those events and encounters had shaped my personality and sense of identity.

Inevitably, questions about the relationship between family history and personal identity continued to arise while I tried to trace my father and, hopefully, his family and forebears. The indication that this research also had potential to illuminate and generate new insights – showing how, when pursued in depth, genealogical research is capable of yielding much more than abstract family trees – was one of the more surprising revelations.

When I embarked on the search for my father, the eventual outcome was quite uncertain. Even much later, when some progress had been made, I never thought that one day the findings might be more widely shared. The turning point was marked by the gradual realisation that the obstacles I was encountering were not personal, but widely shared by other war children with a similar interest in tracing paternal roots. Many, if not most, had discovered that the Canadian authorities were unlikely to welcome their enquiries. Only the most limited assistance was available, leading them to abandon their searches. Access to the necessary records was restricted to those with Canadian citizenship. 'Fortress Canada' was deploying its access to information and privacy legislation as firewalls to block enquiries.

In fairness, my research revealed that, in a very small minority of cases, successful outcomes had been achieved by war children who sought assistance from Project Roots and The Association of Liberation Children, two voluntary agencies that were established with the specific aim of helping Canada's war children make contact with their fathers. For many more though, overtures were unsuccessful and were 'left on file'. My case fell into the even smaller category of those who opted to shun 'official channels' and 'go it alone', using the Internet and sources already in the public realm that were not subject to the same legislative defences. It was to my advantage that the name disclosed after my mother passed away was comparatively uncommon.

If this account of the search for my father were to be regarded as yet another contribution to the misery memoir genre, the sharing of the story will have missed its target. Its aim is not to elicit sympathy, but rather to be an illustrative case study from which lessons might be learned about Canada's apparent disregard of its war children, if not the plight of children born in similar circumstances more generally. As enquiries progressed, as information was gathered about the experiences of other war children and the response of the Canadian authorities, those findings became associated with a burgeoning sense that the war children have been subjected to a discriminatory policy which has deprived them of their basic human right to knowledge about their fathers and paternal roots and, hence, their own identity. In short, they have been denied natural justice.

The more that injustice came to light, the more it rankled. And the more it rankled, the more convinced I became that Canada's treatment of the war children merited closer scrutiny, particularly since it seemed so much at odds with the country's wider record and otherwise deserved reputation in the field of human rights. Through their paternal links, their 'blood ties', the war children are part of Canada's diaspora, the world-wide dispersion beyond its frontier of people with Canadian nationality or genetic inheritance. But while recent legislation has retroactively acknowledged such ties in the case of other categories of 'Lost Canadians', the war children remain excluded from consideration, primarily – and, in my view, mistakenly – because of a persisting failure to provide the assistance to meet their need for information without breaching the country's law on citizenship, privacy, and access to information.

Since Canada's original (and subsequently unrevised) disavowal of any responsibility for its war children in 1946, it has ratified the United Nations International Covenant on Civil and Political Rights and the United Nations Convention on the Rights of the Child. While Article 26 of the covenant asserts the right of all persons to equality before the law; prohibits discrimination and guarantees equal and effective protection against discrimination on various grounds, including national or social origin and/or birth, Article 8 of the convention is yet more explicit. It states:

1. Parties undertake to respect the right of the child to preserve his or her identity, including nationality, name and family relations as recognised by law without unlawful interference.
2. Where a child is illegally deprived of some or all of the elements of his or her identity, parties shall provide appropriate assistance and protection, with a view to speedily re-establishing his or her identity.

The reader may wish to judge the extent to which, if at all, Canada's attitude towards its war children, and its persisting reluctance to provide more help with their searches, contravene the spirit, if not the letter, of those universally recognised, fundamental human rights.

For my part, from obstacles identified in my own search and understanding the disappointment of others who have failed to trace fathers and paternal kith and kin, and from consideration of factors which might explain the disdainful stance the Canadian authorities have adopted over the years, the impression gained is that policy has been guided more by narrow-minded, self-serving motives than any trace of humanitarian concern. It is a blemish on the country's record on human rights. Consequently, unless that blemish is removed, any claim Canada may assert to occupancy of high moral ground in this sphere, as symbolised by the establishment in 2010 of the Canadian Museum of Human Rights, will remain tainted, if not fundamentally flawed.

Paul Cornes
February 2012

1

The Dancing Partner

In March 1983, at the invitation of the World Rehabilitation Fund, I undertook a lecture tour of the Eastern Seaboard and midwestern states of the United States. Midway through the tour, I boarded an early afternoon Republic Airlines flight from La Guardia Airport, New York, to Detroit. In its later stages, the flight path passed over Lake Erie. It was a bright, virtually cloudless spring day. From my starboard seat, there were panoramic views over the northern shoreline of the lake from around Port Stanley to the mouth of the Detroit River. It was my first (albeit distant) glimpse of Canada.

I didn't know at the time, but those captivating views of south-western Ontario embraced land on which some of my forebears, immigrants from England and Ireland, settled in the late 1830s. Awareness of that aspect of my ancestry came much later, after my mother's death in June 2001 when, with evident reluctance, one of her sisters told me about my Anglo-Canadian roots.

Before that discovery, I was conscious there had been unspoken issues surrounding my origins. As I grew up, I sensed an element of mystery, particularly since relevant dates did not quite add up. For many years, I believed – or had been allowed to believe – that while I had been born to a single parent, my mother and father had married later, on the latter's return from wartime service in Burma, and that 'loose ends' had been formally tied by legal adoption in my early teenage years.

That history did not trouble me greatly. In retrospect, it shielded me from the stigma of illegitimacy, which had cast a shadow over the lives of some of my contemporaries. I now know that my birth name was Paul Smith. While I have used the surname Cornes from infant schooldays onward, the addition of my middle name and surname, Frederick Cornes (my adoptive father's name), was the outcome of the legal adoption procedure.

As for my true identity, it emerged after my mother's death that her response to the anxiety she had experienced over my conception and birth led her to keep information about my parentage concealed from me for the remainder of her life. Her 'protectiveness' even went as far as ensuring that my original birth certificate, the legal adoption papers and, it seems, some wartime mementos that might have contained clues about my biological father's identity, could not be found.

However self-centred my mother's actions may now appear to have been, I respect her entitlement to have made those decisions. I also respect the loyalty of those – including my adoptive father, my maternal grandparents and my mother's sisters – who remained faithful to them, sharing in a subterfuge maintained over almost sixty years. However, their loyalty deprived me of information about my origins and awareness of my true ancestry – my identity – together with any chance of establishing contact with my biological father.

At first, I was shocked but not particularly concerned to follow up the information that came to light after my mother's demise. More generally, its disclosure actually seemed to be a source of relief to some relatives, like the release of a safety valve. Not least my adoptive father, who clearly welcomed the lifting of the burden of secrecy to which he had been held. As he put it: 'I'm just glad there'll be no more damned secrets.' Nevertheless, despite the initial reluctance to take matters further, the more I dwelt on those emerging details, the more important it became to establish the truth about my origins and so provide myself, my children and my grandchildren with a more authentic account of our shared ancestry than we had previously been permitted.

My mother, Margaret Kate (Smith) Cornes, was born in the Cambridgeshire village of Burwell in July 1923. She was from a smallholder/farming family, the oldest of four daughters. She was a devoted parent and grandparent, loved and respected by her children (I have a half-sister from the marriage of my mother and adoptive father) and four granddaughters.

Those who recall relevant events told me that, around the time of my conception in the autumn of 1943, she was 'seeing' a young Canadian serviceman, described as her 'dancing partner', who was in the habit of visiting her family home and escorting her to local dances. Their relationship lasted several weeks, possibly two to three months, before he was moved to a new posting, but may not have continued thereafter. It is not known for certain if he was informed about the pregnancy, although one of my maternal aunts believed he might have been. In any event, when my grandfather sought to trace that young man, he was advised – or so it is recalled – that he had been 'sent away'. The serviceman concerned, my biological father, was remembered as Max or 'Maxie' Clements.

The search

Armed with no more than that name and the indication that he was a Canadian serviceman, most probably in the army, I eventually embarked on the quest to trace my father in March 2005. It soon became apparent that little or no assistance could be expected from the Canadian authorities. Canada's Privacy Act and Access to Information Act, both of which allow access to official records only to persons with Canadian citizenship, imposed insuperable obstacles to direct enquiries. Currently, foreign-born illegitimate offspring of Second World War veterans are denied access to personal information (e.g. service records). Even for Canadian citizens, formal proof of death and proof of relationship are required before access to records is granted and, even then, not fully before the twentieth anniversary of the veteran's death.

That official *impasse* left two options. One would have entailed seeking help from specialist voluntary tracing agencies like Project

Roots or The Association of Liberation Children, both of which have well-deserved reputations for the parts they have played in uniting some war children and their Canadian fathers. The other option was to pursue my enquiries independently, making use of secondary sources already available in the public realm. That was the course I chose to follow – not least because I was determined to avoid the obstacles that had caused disappointment for so many of the war children who had conducted their enquiries through officially approved channels.

The first concern was that Max Clements might not have survived the war. However, an examination of the Canadian Department of Veterans Affairs' virtual war memorial revealed that no-one with that or a closely similar name had been posted as missing or killed in action.

The next priority was to narrow the scope of the enquiry, if at all possible. I surmised that, as a veteran, Max Clements might have had some association with the Royal Canadian Legion. A review of their website located its 'Magazine' pages, within which there was a 'Last Post' section. A search revealed a report of the death of a Max H. Clements, formerly a private in the Petrol Company of the Royal Canadian Army Service Corps (RCASC), part of the 4th Canadian Armoured Division. He had passed away aged seventy-four years on 12 June 1999 (two years to the day before my mother's death) in Corunna, Ontario. Further searching located a website for the Royal Canadian Legion Leslie Sutherland Branch 447 in Corunna, where I found that he had been made a life member and that his wife, Selena, had also for a time served as president of its Auxiliary (women's section).

I sought an obituary for Max H. Clements. Though unsuccessful, the search led to a richer vein of similar notices in the press and on funeral home websites, where obituaries of one of his older sisters and two sisters-in-law on his wife's side were found. When linked with cemetery records, those sources provided a tentative outline of his family circle. It was established that Max H. Clements had been interred at Hillsdale Cemetery, Petrolia, about a dozen miles east of

Corunna, and that other family members, including a son, Michael (who had predeceased him), and his parents had also been interred there. The obituary notices for his sister and sisters-in-law suggested he was one of six siblings, three of whom had died with the other two possibly still alive, but living more distantly in British Columbia and New Jersey. All other family members, however, appeared to have spent their lives in or around Petrolia – a community founded in association with the discovery and exploitation of oil reserves in southwestern Ontario in the mid-nineteenth century.

Despite the excitement generated by those early findings, there was still no evidence to link Max H. Clements with my mother. Canadian legislation precluded access to a service record that would confirm his whereabouts around the time of my conception. The alternative was to trace and review Canadian military history records, in particular those relating to the deployment of the 4th Canadian Armoured Division, to which Max H. Clements' RCASC Company had been attached.

The primary sources, a series of reports prepared during or soon after the war by the London-based Historical Section, Canadian Military Headquarters, revealed that the 4th Canadian Armoured Division, which eventually numbered around 700 officers and 14,500 other ranks, underwent preliminary training in Canada in 1941–42. The division was then transported to the United Kingdom via sailings from Halifax, Nova Scotia in four movements in July, August, September and October 1942, before onward transfer to Aldershot, where it established its headquarters and commenced a programme of field training.

In the spring of 1943, the division moved to Heathfield, Sussex, where training was stepped up and it participated in a number of exercises in the southeast of England. On 4 August 1943 it moved to Norfolk, making its headquarters at Cockley Cley (near Swaffham) and took part in other exercises in the Thetford area. On 1 October 1943, new headquarters were established nearby in Suffolk, where the division participated in further exercises including 'Grizzly II' in October and 'Bridoon' in early November 1943. There was no evidence that other Canadian forces were stationed in East Anglia at that time.

After 'Bridoon', the 4th Canadian Armoured Division returned to Sussex. It did not take part in the D-Day landings. However, in July 1944, it crossed the English Channel and was engaged in various actions in France, Belgium and the Netherlands before crossing the River Ems into Germany. After Germany's surrender in May 1945, the division returned to the Netherlands to await its disbandment at the end of the year when, presumably, Max H. Clements was amongst the Canadians who made their way home.

Those previously disparate lines of enquiry seemed to coalesce in placing Max H. Clements within just a few miles of my mother's wartime locality at or around the date of my conception (after a full term pregnancy, I was born in July 1944). But that still did not provide a basis for causal inference about my paternity. The link could have been no more than a coincidence. The person identified may not have been the only member of the 4th Canadian Armoured Division of that or a closely similar name. It seemed that, unless the records (e.g. attestation papers) of Canadian servicemen who served in the Second World War were placed in the public realm, a development that was unlikely to happen for another twenty years, the trail I had followed with mounting hope over the previous six months had ended in a *cul-de-sac*.

My disappointment was soon replaced by fresh optimism after my mother's three younger sisters suggested that, even after sixty-two years, they might still be able to recognise a photograph of the Max Clements who had visited their wartime home. But that possibility raised other issues about what approach to adopt.

Because of persisting uncertainty over whether the 4th Canadian Armoured Division's ranks included more than one person of that name, a direct approach to putative family members was ruled out, since it could have been too intrusive and most probably unwelcome. Instead, I decided to pursue a less direct route. Photographs of Max H. Clements' wife, Selena, on the Royal Canadian Legion's Corunna branch website, suggested that the Legion or the local press in Corunna could be a source of a picture to show to my aunts. The thought occurred of using a local private investigator to trace any such photographic evidence. So, after careful consideration, I drafted a briefing paper in October 2005 outlining the background and the relevant facts. After an initial exchange to establish their interest in taking on the assignment, the briefing paper was forwarded independently to two Canadian private investigation firms.

In the event, neither private investigator produced any evidence. In one case, I doubted that any enquiries were made. In the other, there was interim feedback that a chaplain attached to the Corunna branch of the Royal Canadian Legion had been approached with a request for assistance, but from whom no further information was forthcoming beyond a suggestion that my enquiries could be pursued with Project Roots, an option which had already been discounted. The private investigators were advised that their services were no longer needed. The only positive outcome from the intervening six months was that it had stimulated an interest in discovering more about my ancestry, both maternal and paternal. That interval allowed the opportunity to start to piece together an account of my maternal forebears, a task initially driven by a desire to acquire the expertise to undertake a similar review of Canadian sources, if or when my father's identity was confirmed.

I now know that the Royal Canadian Legion chaplain's response to the private investigator's overtures was probably guided by his awareness that Max H. Clements' widow, Selena, was still alive. From Hillsdale Cemetery records, I had concluded – wrongly – that she too was deceased. (This was because I was unaware of the Canadian custom of inscribing the names of both the deceased and the living on family memorial stones.) It would seem that, with every justification, the chaplain had acted out of pastoral concern to protect her from what could have been construed as insensitive and potentially upsetting enquiries.

I discovered that Selena was still alive later, in March 2006. At that time, almost one year to the day after embarking on the quest, all other avenues of enquiry having been unproductive, I decided to risk a more direct approach. After considerable soul searching and a review of the information about Max H. Clements that had already been assembled, I telephoned Beth Kewley, one of his nieces, the daughter of one of his deceased older sisters. The aim was to identify myself, explain my reasons for getting in touch and request her help with my enquiries. Her response – in the course of which I learned that her Aunt Selena was still living, albeit in poor health – while both courteous and understanding, was also appropriately guarded. It was agreed that I should send her the briefing paper I had prepared for the private investigators, some photographs and the details of two contacts in the nearby city of Sarnia who, quite fortuitously, had been guests at my daughter Emma's wedding and who could vouch for my identity.

The result was an email on 21 May 2006 with an attached photograph of Max H. Clements in uniform, most probably taken around the time of his enlistment and before his division sailed to the United Kingdom. Within a few days, the photograph had been shared with my aunts, two of whom were confidently able to confirm his identity as the young soldier with whom my mother had had a relationship. I had traced the dancing partner. Max H. Clements was my father. I had a new Anglo-Canadian identity with which to come to terms.

Just as my adoptive father devoted much of his later years working voluntarily for the Burma Star Association, the imprint of Max H. Clements' wartime experience led to a life-long involvement in his local Royal Canadian Legion branch. I am pleased he had that affiliation. For, without it, given the Canadian authorities' generally unyielding stance in response to more formal lines of enquiry, he might not have been traced.

Inevitably, confirmation of my father's identity prompted other questions, not only about him and his family but also our shared ancestry. There was no telling when, where or how it might end; the task of tracing them was a journey of discovery on which I embarked with some trepidation. Was Pandora's box about to be opened?

2

A Second Coming?

The photograph of my father marked a significant turning point. My maternal aunts' reactions dispelled any doubt that the Max H. Clements who had been on my radar for fourteen months was my biological father. From its receipt to the year's end, virtually every spare moment was devoted to discovering more about our shared ancestry. The (at times) obsessive pursuit of that objective resulted in the accumulation of a substantial miscellany of literature, print-outs from genealogical websites, notes, jottings and progressively-evolving drafts of my father's family tree. My New Year's resolution for 2007 was to convert it into an orderly account of that side of my family history; to impose some order on that chaotic pile.

The task was initially conceived as an impartial, academic exercise, a marshalling of historical data, but it turned out not to be. Quite soon, it was energised by a more primal force, the urge to connect with the parent I had never met and about whom so very little was known. That desire prompted a second resolution. It was to visit the country of his birth, to see and sense for myself his birthplace and other locations in which he had been raised and spent his life, and pay my respects at his grave.

The desire to learn more about my father, in particular what kind of man he had been, was partly met around one month after his identity was confirmed. A follow-up email from Beth included a brief outline of his post-war life in which she mentioned his involvement as a veteran in Royal Canadian Legion activities, and the loss of his son Michael (my half-brother), tragically killed in a road traffic accident in 1974, aged just seventeen. That much was already known, although not in any detail. The real surprise, truly 'a bolt from the blue', was the reference to a daughter, Marlene. From time to time, it had crossed my mind that Michael might have had a sibling or siblings. But as I had seen nothing to suggest this was the case, I assumed he had been an only child. With hindsight, I realised that Marlene had not been mentioned in the obituary notices of her aunts (the main source of information about my father and his family) because, as a niece of the deceased, she was too distantly related to merit inclusion in lists of principal mourners.

I was spurred on to learn more about my father and newly-disclosed half-sister, about whom only her first name was known. I confessed to Beth my previous ignorance of Marlene's existence and asked her to tell me more. I also asked her to confirm that my paternal grandparents, the link to earlier generations, were Charles and Ethel (Babcock) Clements.

The early response I craved did not come. Rather, a prolonged silence ensued. As the wait became ever longer, there were moments of frustration and apprehension. Had I pushed too hard on the Clements' door? Was I destined to remain outside or was it still ajar, if only marginally? Was there someone or something behind that barrier about whom or about which it had been deemed preferable to keep me in the dark?

Because there was no way of knowing whether such concerns were real or imagined, I settled on a strategy of patient non-intervention. Even though one door might have closed, it was possible another could open. Surely there were other avenues of enquiry that could be pursued without unwanted intrusion into my father's immediate family's space. After all, the family tree had other branches.

Amid those doubts and uncertainties, I realised that I had failed to appreciate as fully as I should the extent of my indebtedness to Beth. To make amends, I posted a Christmas card. It was an opportunity to express a genuinely-felt gratitude for the crucial role she had played in the search for my father. The card was dispatched as a token of closure, of acceptance that after seven months of silence, the Clements' door had been bolted, and was likely to remain so. I diverted my attention to other potential lines of enquiry and resolved to put down on paper the information uncovered so far. Last but not least, there were the burgeoning plans my wife Fay and I were making for a tour of Canada that would include a visit to the area in which my paternal forebears settled and where my father had spent most of his life.

Quite unexpectedly, at the end of January 2007, Beth was back in touch. Both she and her husband John had needed treatment for significant health problems, and had also been preoccupied with the construction of, and move into, a new home. Marlene and her mother had been guests at a family gathering over the Christmas period when a photograph had been taken, which she would forward in due course. I told her I would be intrigued to see it. We now had firm arrangements to visit Canada, including a visit to south-western Ontario, so I ventured the suggestion that we could arrange to meet on neutral ground.

Once again, time passed without any response. After yet another seven months, with less than four weeks to go before our departure date, I decided to follow up the unanswered email. I told Beth about our hotel reservation in Sarnia, and invited her and her husband to be our guests for dinner on one of our evenings there. As so much time had elapsed since we were last in touch, I had little confidence the proposed meeting would take place. I was resigned to the possibility that no more would be learned about either my father or Marlene.

By coincidence, that sense of impending disappointment was offset by a new development. Around the time the Christmas card had been sent to Beth, keen to open other lines of enquiry, I had trawled an online telephone directory for people with other surnames from the family tree who were listed as residents of Newbury, my father's birthplace and the location in which his Clements and Armstrong forebears had settled. That fishing exercise identified an Armstrong who was listed with initials but no indication of gender. I sent a speculative letter briefly outlining my line of descent from Alexander Armstrong (senior), and enquired if they shared those antecedents.

In that case also, several months elapsed without a reply, leading me to conclude I had drawn a blank. So I was quite surprised when, only a few weeks before the departure date of our tour, a reply was delivered to my inbox. My correspondent informed me that she was an Armstrong (by marriage), but not related, and had only recently moved to Newbury. After first setting my letter aside, it had later aroused her curiosity to the extent of sharing its content with others, including the local librarian, Diana Watson. A pamphlet on the history of Newbury in which there were references to the Armstrong family had been posted to me.

I thanked my Armstrong correspondent for her kindness and assistance and mentioned that my forebears also included members of the Watson and Babcock families. A subsequent exchange opened up new lines of communication with the librarian's husband, John Watson, with whom it was discovered I share descent from William and Alexander Watson (our respective great grandparents were brother and sister), and Joe Babcock, with whom I share descent from Joseph and Elizabeth (Watson) Babcock. Joe's father and my paternal grandmother were also siblings. So although my speculative enquiry had not located an Armstrong, its serendipitous outcome led to two other ancestral lines. Meetings with those newly-found, albeit more distant relatives were arranged before setting off for Canada.

There was one more twist. It came in the form of two 'eleventh hour' emails from Beth. The first indicated acceptance of the invitation to meet in Sarnia. The second, received just a week before our departure, reported that she and her Aunt Wanda (the widow of my father's older brother) had visited Marlene and her mother in Corunna the previous day, when Marlene had been taken to one side and told she had a half-brother. She had also been informed about our visit and invited to the previously arranged meeting. What passed through Beth's mind in the days before her visit to Corunna, let alone throughout the eighteen months since my initial telephone call, was unimaginable. For it appeared she had mainly kept her own counsel, possibly confiding in her innermost family circle, but not beyond.

The journey

Seated in the departure lounge at Glasgow Airport on 16 September 2007, awaiting the boarding call for our Zoom Airline flight to Toronto, my own mind was also in a state of flux, a rapidly-alternating mix of expectation and trepidation. Taking stock, I felt reasonably well prepared for what might lie in store. My hand luggage contained the most recent draft of the account of my paternal ancestry, on which I had worked assiduously since the New Year, its inclusion a totemic passport for the journey into a previously unknown family hinterland. Aware that the draft was incomplete, there was also a substantial file comprising lists of questions to which answers had yet to be found and information about people, events and dates that still needed to be established. The file also included contact details for people and places I planned to visit to remedy gaps in my knowledge; numerous maps and copies of cemetery records; and the itinerary that hopefully would ensure my information-gathering objectives would be achieved.

In other ways, I felt much less well prepared. The journey ahead was more than a one-off, fact-gathering mission. It was just the latest stage in a psychological safari that had begun well before that morning's drive to the airport. There was no certainty about where, when or how that longer journey would end, or what I might learn on the way. Earlier, when further contact with my father's immediate family circle seemed unlikely, I had expected (and was prepared to accept) that the visit to his grave would bring closure to my quest. But that scenario had been disrupted by the most recent communications from Canada. The outcome of the impending meeting with Beth (and Marlene, if she came) was not predictable. If it ended unfavourably, would it matter? How would I cope with rejection, if it came to that?

For all the planning and preparation, I was about to enter a land of strangers, about whom very little was known. Take my father, for instance. My investigations had revealed much more about his forebears than him and his close family. I didn't know what the middle 'H' stood for in his name. I knew the date on which he died, but not his date of birth. Official records had given me a broad outline of his military service, but nothing was known about his wartime experience, or what prompted him to volunteer for active service when he would have been no older than eighteen years (it was later revealed that he was only sixteen when he enlisted and that he had lied about his age). The only photograph I had seen dated from that time. It had been established that he returned to Canada after the war, when he married and raised a family of two children, Michael who had died tragically young and Marlene who was still alive. They were my half-siblings. I knew their names, but little else. I had been informed that my father spent his working life in the local petrochemical industry, but had learned nothing about his education or career.

The draft in my hand luggage had concluded that the review of family history had resulted in both rewarding and disappointing outcomes. Rewards included the revelation of a heritage about which, until quite recently, I had no prior knowledge. I had a growing sense of connectedness with a Canadian past and the people who populated it. I was disappointed with the persisting lack of insight into the kind of man my father had been in terms of character, personality and accomplishments, but retained hope that opportunities would arise to learn more about him. Nonetheless, I knew that the genealogical quest, which had given me a broad sense of family rather than any feeling of familiarity with my father and his close kin, might not take me beyond the picture that had already been revealed.

The equilibrium of that position was short-lived. It had been disturbed by Beth's change of mind (if that is what it was), and the prospect that the journey would not end at my father's grave but in a meeting with living relatives, including my half-sister. Thoughts turned to Marlene. Whereas I had been aware of her existence for some time, it was only a week or two since she had been obliged to deal with the intrusion into her life of a hitherto unknown half-brother. How had she reacted? Would knowledge of my existence mar her perception of her late father? Would we meet or remain estranged? If we did meet, would she be willing to share memories of her father? How old was she? Was she married and, if so, what was her surname? Were there children, grandchildren? Where did she live? What was she like – not only in terms of personality, but also appearance (the promised photograph had not been received), interests, education and life experience? There were so many unknowns.

This led me to confront the extent to which the emotional dimension of my journey had been put on ice, if not repressed. Tears shed after my mother's passing had been more of rage and anguish than grief. Grieving her loss, appreciation of her many positive attributes and qualities took longer. In similar vein, the search for my father had been construed as an essentially dispassionate exercise in historical research. In retrospect, that guise had allowed the erection of a protective barrier between my 'subject' and me. But contemplation of the turmoil that potentially laid in wait on arrival in Canada stripped away any lingering traces of that veneer. It had been right to defer the meeting in Sarnia to our penultimate evening there. It should buy time to prepare myself emotionally. Under the worst case scenario of rejection, the days leading up to that meeting should at least provide opportunities to secure the fallback position of gathering some, if not all, of the family history information I still wished to obtain.

Meetings

All went reasonably well with the flight to Toronto, but after an anxious wait to check in, our connection to Sarnia was delayed. We arrived just before the airport was about to close for the night with not a single taxi in sight. We checked into our hotel just before midnight, thanks to our flight crew who asked their driver to summon a taxi for us.

The next morning, our first objective was to locate my father's grave. After picking up the rental car, we set off for Petrolia. Fay was driving and I was navigating. It was surprising to note how many of the fields had been converted to paddocks for horses. The healthy sheen on their coats seemed a poor recompense for the toil of earlier generations who drained swamps and cleared forest and bush to create those fields.

Hillsdale was the first of the well-maintained cemeteries we were to visit. A couple of miles west of Petrolia, it had gently undulating grounds in which older plots were shaded by mature woodland. The area was huge and we assumed the grave would be hard to find. A member of the grounds staff couldn't help us, but did direct us to Petrolia Town Hall, where an obliging employee gave us a copy of a plan on which my father's and his parents' final resting places were marked.

The grave was an unprepossessing memorial. It comprised a small, rectangular, granite block, on which my father's name and years of birth and death were inscribed alongside similar details for my half-brother Michael. The stone also bore his wife's name and date of birth – the detail that had led me to believe she was also buried there. To one side, there was a Royal Canadian Legion memorial marker in the shape of a maple leaf with the simple acknowledgement: 'He served his country'. Apart from a small posy of artificial flowers, there was no other ornamentation.

As I stood by the grave in a stillness disturbed only by a background chorus of chirruping insects, with the early autumn sun warming my back and with Fay, respectful of the moment, graciously keeping in the background, my first reaction was a sense of guilt that I was not adding my own floral tribute to that memorial. It was not an oversight, but reflected a still ongoing concern to refrain from any gesture my father's family might perceive as intrusive or unwanted. Nor did I feel any immediate sense of loss or grief; that was to come later. Rather, that proximity to his remains engendered an overwhelming sense of communion, of having connected in spirit if not in life.

Until that moment, I would not have considered that I had a

particularly sentimental disposition. Yes, there had been times at funerals when I had struggled to stem an upwelling of tears, but those responses had been quite fleeting. The visit to Hillsdale had a different effect. As we drove from the cemetery, I was aware that, while my father and I could never be closer physically, I was leaving with a sense of attachment, of having bonded, that would span an ocean.

From Petrolia, we headed for Wyoming, to visit the local history archive at Lambton County Library, before travelling on to Alvinston to locate the grave of my great grandparents, Thomas and Mary Ann (Armstrong) Clements. Afterwards, despite the jet lag we were experiencing, Fay agreed to a suggestion that the return route to Sarnia should include Corunna, the small town in which my father had spent his later years. Impelled by curiosity, and guided by a map downloaded from the Internet during a speculative online search of an international telephone directory for a Clements listing, we drove along Fane Street. Fay was first to spot the property for which we were looking. But such was my state of mind that, by the time her report registered, we had driven past. After a couple of blocks, she turned the car round, instructing me to concentrate and look more carefully. And so I did.

We lingered in Corunna for the next hour or so, basking in the early evening sun, enjoying the view from the town's jetty across the St Clair River to Stag Island. We didn't realise at the time, but in that spot we were only a few yards from the house in which my father actually lived before his death. The Fane Street property we had tracked down was one to which his widow had moved afterwards. Fay's journal entry for that day concluded: 'Early night. Paul emotionally exhausted and both of us feeling dead tired through lack of sleep.'

With foreboding over the meeting in Sarnia never far from my mind, the next two days were mainly spent in Southwest Middlesex, criss-crossing the highways and dirt road byways of Mosa Township. We located the lot on which William Clements settled and the nearby rail crossing on which the fatal accident involving his son Thomas, my great grandfather, occurred. We visited Oakland Cemetery, where Babcock and Watson forebears were interred, and also the Armstrong and Robinson family plots at Wardsville Old Cemetery. A stopover in Newbury allowed me to thank personally the (unrelated) Armstrong contact who had put me in touch with John Watson and Joe Babcock.

With their wives, Diana and Myrtle, John and Joe warmly welcomed us to their homes, where we received generous hospitality and listened to lively anecdotes and reminiscences about earlier generations. John had a fund of stories about the Watson family's migration from Ompah. Joe, a sprightly, mentally alert octogenarian, is my father's first cousin. They grew up together in Newbury and were life-long friends. He had much to tell, both then and in the telephone conversations that were to follow. I shall never forget his words of welcome, looking me up and down as I crossed his threshold: 'There's no doubt about it. You're Max's son.' He was not alone in spotting how closely I resembled my father in looks and build.

As restricted opening hours meant that the Glencoe and District Historical Society's records would only be available on the day we were to meet my Clements relatives, Fay and I had time to indulge in some local sightseeing. We selected a route through Elgin County, where we glimpsed the vastness of Lake Erie from the yacht club at Port Glasgow. On the return journey, we paused at the bridge over the Thames River, south of Wardsville. Looking east, there was a view of the Big Bend Conservation Area, a protected tract of pre-settlement landscape, the original 'Skunks Misery' (the somewhat disparaging term residents of Newbury and its environs have adopted when referring to the area in which they live).

On returning to the hotel from Glencoe, tension mounted. I tried to study the afternoon's 'treasure trove' – copies of John Robinson's will and the quitclaim deed for the estate of Alexander Armstrong (senior), who died intestate, which Harold Carruthers, the society's volunteer curator, had made for me – but could not concentrate. Perceiving my anxiety, Fay counselled it was probably not the occasion for a nerve-steadying drink; it was sound advice.

My cousin and her husband were expected to arrive at 7.00 p.m. To avoid the discourtesy of not being on hand to greet them, we posted ourselves in the reception area ahead of schedule. The appointed hour came... and went. Had they decided against coming? When they did arrive, only ten minutes late (it seemed longer), Beth and John were most apologetic. It transpired they had been on time, but had mistakenly driven to a neighbouring hotel. Beth, it seemed, was just as apprehensive about our meeting as I had been. But where was Marlene? Apparently, she was intending to join us if or when cover was arranged for her mother, whose round-the-clock care needs meant she could not be left unattended.

Though preconceptions can be misleading, in Beth's case they were not. Her personality and demeanour reflected the image I had formed from previous telephone calls and our exchange of emails. Modest, reserved, introspective, conscientious, generally conservative in outlook and opinion, with a sharp mind, commonsense approach to life, strong commitment to home and family, and a passion for quilt making, she epitomised that image of a Women's Institute member from 'jam and Jerusalem' days. She had been the linchpin in the search for my father, performing a role that may not have been entirely voluntary and that was probably the source of much soul searching. However, the task could not have been entrusted to a better person. I remain ever grateful for all she did.

After introducing ourselves, we found seating from which we could keep an eye on the entrance. From an initially faltering conversation, it emerged that Beth had been unable to download fully the photographs I had sent. Only a small fragment had printed out. Nonetheless, it had been sufficient to discern that my father and I were of similar appearance and to convince Beth that my claim to relationship was most probably genuine. Conversation turned to our respective families. Both she and John were from local farming families whose forebears had arrived in Upper Canada before 1850. They had also spent their working lives in agriculture – although, in common with other farmers with modest holdings, John had worked in local industry to supplement their income. They had raised a family of four, two sons and two daughters, all now in adulthood.

The anxiety and trepidation Beth and I shared evaporated within seconds of Marlene's arrival, accompanied by her husband, Byron. She embraced me immediately. Her first words were: 'So you're Paul, I guess I have to call you brother.' They were quickly followed by the challenge: 'By the way, did you drive past my house the other evening?' While I was slow to respond, thinking that I didn't know where she lived, Fay's antennae quickly detected that the question referred to our supposedly discreet drive up and down Fane Street in Corunna two days previously. Answering on my behalf, she confirmed we had been there. We had been spotted because we had not been aware that Marlene lived across the street from her mother. (We really ought to have appreciated that the eye-catching, brilliant white Chevrolet Cobalt we had rented was likely to have attracted attention in any neighbourhood.) Marlene's never-to-be-forgotten account of her reaction was hilarious: 'My God, I thought, that's Dad in that car... and there he is again... I'm so glad Mother isn't looking out... she'd think it's the second coming!'

Ice broken, and with Beth perceptibly relieved (me less so), conversation flowed throughout dinner, with no awkward silences. Fay and I fretted that the service was abysmally slow and inattentive, but our guests seemed not to mind. After the meal, we claimed a corner of the lounge, where another surprise awaited. Marlene had 'smuggled' a well-worn family album from her mother's home to bring to our meeting. At the top of the very first page was a photograph of my father and Bob Govier, his army comrade, that had been taken in Burwell. They were posing beneath a sign advertising Sandeman Ports at the front entrance of the White Horse Hotel in the village High Street. It was an all-too-familiar scene, marking a spot I had passed daily on my way to and from school between the ages of five and eleven.

A blur of photographs and anecdotes, the remainder of that first meeting passed quickly. Photographs were taken to commemorate the occasion and Marlene and I parted with an agreement to get together the following evening. Fay and I were left with a selection of family photographs and directions to a shop where they could be copied.

Marlene and Byron arrived for the second meeting laden with more albums and several boxes. When emptied onto our hotel room bed, the boxes were found to contain a miscellany of cuttings, documents relating to *our* (that descriptor was now 'official') father's military service, badges, medals and other memorabilia. To my acute embarrassment, Marlene insisted they were to be shared. As we were booked on an early Via Rail service to Toronto the following morning, there was a second, more frantic visit to get yet more copying done before the shop's late evening closing time. On parting, we vowed to keep in touch, neither one doubting the permanence of our newly-forged bond.

The four and a half hour journey to Toronto afforded respite from the hurly-burly of preceding days and gave me time to reflect. So much had happened and changed. Before setting off for Canada, I would have been content with opportunities to pay respects at my father's grave, visit the locations where he was born and spent his life, and fill in some gaps in family history. Meeting family members would have been a bonus. As an interloper, I had been prepared for the possibility that my introduction to the family circle could be met with caution, suspicion, even polite rejection, but not the warmth and spontaneity of the welcome I actually received. I was leaving the area in which my paternal forebears had settled with an embryonic kinship network that in the following months Marlene was to ensure would expand to embrace an ever-increasing number of my 'new' family's members.

Most significantly, there was Marlene herself, who had become much more than a name. Like Maggie, the half-sister with whom I was raised, Marlene was part of the post-war baby boom, the offspring of fathers who were demobilised on return from overseas service in 1946. Her first marriage, during which two daughters were born (one a year older, the other a year younger than my two), had ended in divorce. Her second marriage to Byron, a widower with two young sons, created a family of four children who, in turn, produced eleven grandchildren. All live locally and are frequent visitors to their Grandma and Poppa's home.

From the time the existence of my Canadian half-sister was first disclosed, I had often wondered what she was like. It did not take long to find out. The main cues were clearly evident in her first, ice-breaking appearance. Marlene has an astute, easy-going, self-assured, extraverted demeanour within which the most prominent attributes are warmth, sociability, candour and generosity. Her conversation, punctuated by nervous laughter, has an empathic quality. It reflects an ability to put a listener at ease, of establishing rapport, which most probably was honed in the 'confessional' atmosphere of the family's beauty and hairdressing salon in which she worked for a time alongside her mother. Above all, though, Marlene possesses that intuitive, matter-of-fact, down-to-earth grasp of situations and circumstances that, while far from unique to her gender, is rarely found in men.

Undoubtedly, it was the latter quality that enabled Marlene to come to terms with the news that she had a half-brother and decide upon her response within a few days. In reading about the experiences of others born in similar circumstances who have tried to trace their Canadian fathers, the crucial role that female relatives played in successful outcomes, in making room for another place at the family table, is very evident. The annals of Project Roots, on its website and in *Voices of the Left Behind* – the book its founders, Olga and Lloyd Rains, have co-authored with Melynda Jarratt – include numerous examples in which half-sisters, aunts and female cousins were instrumental in the formation and maintenance of links between those who were left behind and their paternal kin. Those sources do include some cases in which fathers' responses were favourable, and a minority in which fathers rather than their children initiated searches. For the most part, though, enquiries addressed directly to fathers appear to have been met by a mixture of evasion, denial and shelter behind the official barrier of Canada's privacy and access to information legislation. The negative tone of those responses had been set in 1946 by the Canadian Government's disavowal of responsibility for unmarried partners of its country's servicemen and their children, even when paternity had been formally acknowledged.

My father died a few weeks before my fifty-fifth birthday, my mother two years later. I have often wondered what his response would have been if my efforts to trace him had begun during his lifetime. Marlene and others have spoken reassuringly, implying he would have accepted me into his family. But that is conjecture and will remain so. Not only did I not know about my paternity while my mother was alive, but also there is no way of knowing with any certainty either that he would have been traced at that earlier time or, if he was, how he would have resolved the conflict that might have resulted from my unexpected appearance in his otherwise settled life.

Though inevitably disappointed that fate determined we would never meet as father and son, his legacy of a kinship network, past and present, is inestimable. In particular, there is the living link with Marlene. Those who knew my father have observed that we have inherited his stockiness (reportedly a 'Babcock' characteristic). In other respects, despite our half-sibship, it might be held that we are chalk and cheese. Whereas it has been my good fortune to have inherited some readily recognisable features and mannerisms, Marlene – who shares her mother's appearance – has undoubtedly inherited aspects of our father's temperament and personality.

After returning from Canada, contact with Marlene continued with weekly telephone calls. There was so much to talk about, they seldom lasted less than an hour. They were opportunities to consolidate our bond in an exchange of information and reminiscences about our respective families. In November 2007, two months after our first, clandestine meeting, Marlene's mother died, followed by my adoptive father two months later. Grief over the loss of those two 'innocent parties' was shared. Neither had been told about our meeting. At the time, both had been experiencing rapidly-declining health. Rightly or wrongly, we did not want our news to overshadow or impair their perceptions and memories of partners with whom they had shared over fifty years of marriage.

Marlene's keenness to introduce me to Canadian relatives, despite the distance between us, was expressed in various ways. There were numerous conversations with her daughters and grandchildren, whose visits to her home just happened to coincide with the pre-arranged times of our telephone calls. She also ensured that contact was made with my father's younger sister. Aunt Shirley, who lives in New Jersey, extended a warm welcome and has since made it her business, through a series of detailed letters and telephone calls, to tell me about my paternal grandparents, in particular their family backgrounds, the ups and downs of their lives, and the home life they provided for their children. As she was still at home throughout the war, Aunt Shirley has also been the main source of insights into my father's boyhood, enlistment and military service. Marlene has provided other glimpses into my father's past. Her trawling has also yielded an album of photographs of the extended family. Most appreciated and most moving of all was her gift of a videotaped collage of cine film footage featuring my father at different stages of his life from his enlistment in 1941, through his family life in the intervening years, to his golden wedding celebration in 1996.

As a student, I learned about the significance of reciprocity as a sustaining force in relationships. Not surprisingly, the imbalanced nature of the exchanges with relatives in Canada became a concern. I welcomed the opportunity to redress that imbalance, if only in small measure, when Marlene and Byron visited my home in Scotland in May 2008. During their stay, I accompanied them to Cambridgeshire. We visited the picturesque estate village of Chippenham, where it is believed our father was billeted, and Burwell, where he met my mother. We paused for a photograph outside the White Horse Hotel, where our father was photographed in 1943, and saw the houses, schools and other places associated with my younger years, including the riverside locations where I fished and swam and the land my maternal grandfather farmed. We paid a visit to Aunt Gina, the youngest of my mother's three sisters, who recalled our father visiting the Smiths' family home. And we met my English half-sister Maggie and her husband, with whom we spent a most convivial evening at a local restaurant.

Travelling on to my daughter Hester's home in Maidenhead, where her sister Emma also joined us, I had the pleasure of introducing them, their partners and my three grandchildren Beth, Toby and Eleanor. It was Marlene's turn to be apprehensive and Toby's role to be the ice-breaker in his spontaneous invitation to 'Auntie Marlene' to join in their games. At the end of that all too short time together, they had been shepherded into her matriarchal fold.

Thereafter, our weekly telephone calls continued and contacts with my Canadian family expanded to include other conversations with my father's sister and two of his first cousins, as well as with an increasing number of other relatives, including some of my own newly-discovered cousins. They were followed by a second visit to Canada, which Fay and I made in May 2010. There were so many highlights. We renewed our acquaintance with Joe and Myrtle Babcock and had the pleasure of meeting members of their family at Joe's eighty-ninth birthday celebration. We also met up again with my cousin Beth and her husband John, and John and Diana Watson (the librarian). With Marlene and Byron, we made 'pilgrimages' to the grave of William Clements in Carson City, Michigan, and also to those of two brothers of his estranged second wife, Margaret (McLear) Clements, in the Old Martyrs' Cemetery in Wardsville. There were also numerous encounters with Byron's sons, Byron (junior) and Bradley, and the latter's sons, and Marlene's daughters, Selena and Maxine, their partners and their children, with all of whom we passed many most enjoyable hours socialising and as spectators at school sports events. The spontaneity and warmth of those welcomes into the family circle and the associated hospitality are treasured memories.

Above all, there was the family reunion at the Royal Canadian Legion's Corunna branch on 30 May, which Marlene had arranged with the help of her daughters, their partners and her grandchildren. Over eighty people were there. Their number included relatives from both the Clements-Armstrong and Babcock-Watson ancestral lines, amongst them my Aunt Shirley, who had travelled with her son from her home in New Jersey especially for the occasion, and my father's first cousin, Kathleen Clements, who has provided much information about the Clements family's history from her personal archive. Other guests included some of Marlene's relatives on her mother's side, some members of Byron's family and other well-wishers, one of whom was the President of the Royal Canadian Legion's Corunna branch. In their different ways, all contributed to making the afternoon a most happy and memorable occasion. There was, however, one ironic twist. On the walls of the Legion's main reception room, there were photographs of my father, one in a prominent display of all past holders of the office of branch President. If the private investigators I instructed in 2005 had been at all diligent, their fees would have been 'easy money'!

My mother and father met in 1943. She was twenty years old and working in an aircraft factory. He was a year or so younger and one of a half-million Canadian servicemen stationed in Britain. Some had been involved in the ill-fated raid on Dieppe the previous year. All were marking time as plans were made to open a second front in Western Europe. It was a year in which the Axis powers suffered reverses on land in North Africa, Italy and Russia; on the high seas, where Germany's U-boats were rendered less effective; and in the air, as overstretched defences became less able to resist the onslaught of allied bombing raids.

Undoubtedly, those world-shaping events were an overwhelming preoccupation for statesmen, military top brass and others whose lives were at risk in the front line. But less so, it might be thought, for younger people, service personnel and civilians alike, who are said to have sought the solace and escapism of the cinema, the dance hall, the public house and the all-too-often brief romantic episodes that ensued in that live-for-the-moment, who-knows-what-tomorrow-will-bring atmosphere. Given their ages and circumstances, it is more than likely that, in their time together, my parents were disinclined to dwell on current events or their family backgrounds and personal histories. So an ironic outcome of these enquiries is that they may have taught me much more about my father and his family than my mother ever knew.

Without any shadow of doubt, the results of my enquiries, the identification of my biological father and acceptance into his family circle, were immensely rewarding. But those outcomes did not provide closure to my quest. Rather, there were three overarching issues that continued to play on my mind. The first concerned my father and our shared ancestry, the half of my family tree about which my mother had been determined to keep me in life-long ignorance. What more was there to learn about my father, his immediate family and our pioneer forebears? The second concerned the reasons for my mother's reluctance to tell me about my father. Had she acted out of purely altruistic concern, from instinctive maternal protectiveness, or had her actions been guided by other motives? The third was Canada's seemingly disdainful treatment of its war children and apparent reluctance to provide meaningful and effective help with their efforts to trace their fathers or paternal kith and kin. Why was that official stance adopted in the first instance and why has it remained unchanged, particularly in the light of more recent measures that recognise other 'Lost Canadians'? Is it really beyond the will and imagination of the Canadian Government to devise and implement a more accommodating solution to its war children's plight?

As background to further consideration of the first two of those issues, brief descriptions follow of the villages of Burwell, Cambridgeshire and Newbury, Mosa Township, Ontario, the two main locations in which events took their course.

3

Locations

At an early stage, the quest to trace my father developed into a much broader enquiry into my ancestry, both English and Canadian. Like Topsy, genealogical research has a seemingly inexhaustible potential for growth. If it is not to become a never-ending obsession, boundaries need to be set.

My research took as its focal points the marriages of my paternal and maternal grandparents. They were Charles Clements and Ethel Rebecca Babcock, who were married in Walkerville, Ontario in 1913, and Arthur George Smith and Kate Bray, who were married in Burwell, Cambridgeshire in 1923. Through information recorded on their marriage certificates, in conjunction with other sources, it was possible to trace generation upon generation of forebears on both sides of the Atlantic. The research identified all of my eight great grandparents, all of my sixteen great great grandparents, and all but two of my thirty-two great great great grandparents. The latter, the parents of my paternal great great grandmother Mary Ann (Kirk) Watson, are thought to have emigrated from their home in County Donegal, but their identities and whereabouts in Upper Canada have yet to be discovered.

While many even older roots have been traced, the following account mainly takes as its baseline ancestors who were born during the reign of George III (1760–1820). To set that baseline in context, George III was crowned one year after General Wolfe's victory at Quebec, a victory that paved the way for the ending of French authority in North America. His reign ended around five years after the defeat of Napoleon Bonaparte's forces at the battle of Waterloo, the event that led to his eventual exile. Between those events, the course of history was marked by the row over taxation between the British Crown and its North American colonies, the prelude to the Boston Tea Party in 1773, which, in turn, precipitated the American War of Independence, and the storming of the Bastille in 1789, which sparked the French Revolution. More generally, George III's reign was marked by the progressively-transforming influences of the so-called Agricultural and Industrial Revolutions, during which Britain developed from an essentially peasant economy into the world's most industrialised society, later to be followed by other countries.

For the most part, my forebears were not amongst those who abandoned the land to work in factories, foundries, mills and mines. Those who remained in Britain mostly kept their roots firmly planted in the countryside. They were obliged to cope with different privations, resulting from the changes in land tenure and farming methods that accompanied the spread of enclosures and applications of 'scientific agriculture', forces that transformed Georgian peasants into the generally impoverished agricultural labourers of the nineteenth century. Others also shunned participation in the emerging industrial society by leaving their homes in England, Ireland and Scotland to take advantage of the opportunities that were increasingly available from around 1820 onward to transplant their rural roots in Upper Canada, as Ontario was then known. Of my sixteen paternal great great great grandparents, only two, the parents of William Clements, spent their entire lives in Britain.

This, then, is essentially a story of country folk. It involves eight main ancestral lines. From my mother's perspective, there are the Smiths of Burwell and the Waymans of Histon, then Cambridge, my maternal grandfather's forebears, and the Brays of Kings Lynn and the Cornwells of Fordham, from whom my maternal grandmother descended. From my father's perspective, there are the Clements from England and the Armstrongs from Ireland, my paternal grandfather's ancestors; and the Watsons from Scotland and the Babcocks, whose English forebears emigrated to the North

American colonies in the 1630s, from whom my paternal grand-mother descended.

Burwell, Cambridgeshire

Burwell lies around 11 miles northeast of Cambridge, 4 miles northwest of Newmarket and around 12 miles southeast of Ely. It is one of a string of 'spring line' villages marking the boundary between the once-waterlogged Fens to the west and north and the formerly densely wooded, higher ground that characterises the Cambridgeshire-Suffolk border to the east and south. Burwell has always been one of the largest parishes in Cambridgeshire, its boundary extending up to 7 miles in one direction and 4 miles in another. Its population is said to have numbered around 800 in the late eighteenth century, increasing to around 1,250 in 1801. During my childhood and youth in the 1950s, the population was thought to number around 2,500. The most recent local authority estimate is that it is about to exceed 6,000.

The place name 'Burwell' is said to derive from Old English terms 'burg' and 'wielle'; fort by the spring. Although mentioned in the Domesday Book, when its population was reported to include fifty peasants and ten serfs, its history spans a much longer period. Traces of a Bronze Age settlement have been found around the village, and there have been several other archaeological finds indicative of Roman and Saxon settlement later on. Indeed, part of the village's southern boundary is marked by the Devil's Ditch, an earthwork defence constructed in or around the sixth century across the ancient route of Icknield Way.

To this day, the village's layout retains the imprint of mediaeval occupation. Although some buildings have been lost or replaced, a manor house, castle site, guildhall, stocks (now recalled only by name), and the last of four windmills (now part of the village museum) are all close to the parish church of St Mary the Virgin in a part of the village known locally as High Town. Other evidence of mediaeval occupation is found beyond High Town, in the remains of other manorial properties, and in the area called Newnham which reportedly was once a 'port'.

In my childhood, Burwell was still a largely agricultural community. I recall my maternal grandfather, who was amongst the last of his generation of local farmers to modernise, taking horses to plough and to haul, using a reaper-binder at harvest, stacking and threshing corn in sheaves, conveying sacks of barley to the windmill for grinding into pig meal, and leading his shires – Kit, Daisy and Violet – to the village blacksmith's premises to be shod. My growing up, however, coincided with the ever-increasing mechanisation of farming and emergence of large agribusinesses which progressively bought out the farmers with smaller holdings, and which now dominate the farming scene in East Anglia.

After I left the village in 1963, its character continued to change. The number of people engaged in agriculture dwindled. Industries based on the manufacture of bricks, fertilisers and corrugated cardboard containers, which once provided alternative employment for some of those displaced from farming, all closed down. The railway station was closed in 1964, one of many casualties of Dr Beeching's axe. There are now fewer shops and public houses. Surrounding meadows have been taken for housing estates and smaller plots have been used for more select developments. Thus, over the past half century, Burwell has shared the fate of so many other formerly thriving villages that have gradually mutated into dormitory communities. For the Smith family's descendants, historic roots and links to the past – their heritage – will finally disappear with the disposal of the last of the land their ancestors farmed alongside the road to Reach.

Newbury, Mosa Township

Around 3,700 miles west of Burwell is the village of Newbury, in what was once Mosa Township, Middlesex County, Ontario, where some of my paternal forebears first settled in the late 1830s and early 1840s. Mosa Township, now part of the municipality of Southwest Middlesex, comprised a triangular tract of land stretching northwards from its southern boundary, marked by the winding course of the Thames River in the southwestern corner of the province. Newbury is located close to the boundary between the counties of Middlesex and Lambton. It is 30 miles southwest of London (Ontario) and around 15 miles inland from the northern shoreline of Lake Erie.

Ontario has only been known by that name since the Dominion of Canada was established by Act of Parliament in 1867. To my ancestors, it would first have been known as Upper Canada. However, around the time they settled in Mosa, the Act of Union, 1841 created a shared assembly (the precursor of the parliament established by the British North America Act, 1867) for Upper and Lower Canada, renaming the former Canada West and the latter (now Quebec) Canada East. Upper and Lower Canada had been created as independent colonies by the Constitutional Act, 1791.

The 1791 legislation was passed in the aftermath of the Declaration of Independence by thirteen former British colonies and the subsequent War of Independence, which led to the formation of the United States of America. It was prompted by the British Crown's need to establish sovereignty over the former territory of New France, which France had ceded to Britain under the Treaty of Paris in 1763 at the end of the Seven Years War. At that time, European settlement in the area that was to become Upper Canada was sparse, a few trappers and fur traders, mostly of French descent, and soldiers manning widely-dispersed forts. First Nation people, the Iroquois to the south and the Huron to the north, who had yet to be displaced from the widespread forests and lakes that covered their traditional tribal lands, were more numerous. Generally, life in Upper Canada in the second half of the eighteenth century was not unlike the picture painted in J. Fenimore Cooper's epic tale, *The Last of the Mohicans*.

It was against that background that Ontario (mainly the south) was settled in three main phases of immigration. The first phase was initially characterised by people crossing the frontier from the United States. That group included the United Empire Loyalists, whose ranks included some of my paternal grandmother's Babcock ancestors, who had stayed loyal to the Crown throughout the American War of Independence and after. They opted to leave the newly-formed United States to settle in Nova Scotia and New Brunswick, along the St Lawrence River and in southeastern Ontario, in and around the Bay of Quinté in the area of what is now Kingston, as well as in the vicinity of Niagara. The settlement of the United Empire Loyalists was facilitated by grants of land of varying size, according to rank, to all who had served the Crown under arms, and later also to their children. The Loyalists were joined by Scottish immigrants, some of whom had been displaced by the Highland clearances.

During the first phase of immigration, the population of Upper Canada increased from around 10,000 in the late 1780s to 77,000 in 1811 and 150,000 in 1824. Within the next decade, the opening of the Erie, Lachine, Welland and Rideau canals facilitated a second wave of settlement inland from the northern shorelines of Lake Ontario and Lake Erie into the hinterland of southeastern and southwestern Ontario.

The second phase of immigration from around 1820 to the early 1840s took place in response to two other main stimuli. One was the continuing pressure to expand settlement and consolidate the Crown's hold over its remaining North American colonies in order to resist the territorial expansion interests of the United States. Taking advantage of Britain's preoccupation with Napoleon Bonaparte's France, the United States had already declared war on Britain in 1812, a conflict that was ended, without modification of the pre-war frontier, by the Treaty of Ghent in 1814. The other stimulus was Britain's need for new policies to deal with two major sources of social and economic distress. The first was mass unemployment amongst the large numbers of former soldiers, whose service was no longer required after the defeat of the French at the Battle of

Waterloo in 1815 brought the Napoleonic Wars to an end. The second source was associated with the even more numerous and rapidly-swelling ranks of agricultural labourers without jobs, or with only seasonal employment on which to rely. Jointly, those two groups were straining the country's parish-based system of poor relief to breaking point.

Thus, even before the amendment of Poor Law legislation in 1834, there was an increasing interest in and encouragement of emigration, with former soldiers offered land grants as inducements, and with others who were without means offered assisted passages and the opportunity to acquire land for which payment would be made on a year-by-year basis once settled. Emigrants from those backgrounds, together with others who possessed the means to travel and settle independently, made their way to Upper Canada in ever-larger numbers. By 1830, its population had increased to 213,000, with further increases to 432,000 by 1840, 952,000 by 1851–52 and 1,396,000 by 1860–61. Amongst that growing population of settlers were my paternal grandfather's Armstrong ancestors from Ireland and Clements and Robinson forebears from England, all of whom settled in Mosa Township between 1837–41.

The third phase of settlement, from around the mid 1840s onwards, was associated with development and expansion of the railroad network and the growth of towns. It was also marked by mass immigration from Ireland, arising from potato crop failures and the resultant Great Famine. The last of my paternal ancestors to settle in Canada, the Turners from County Antrim and the McLears from County Tyrone, were part of that exodus. However, there were other reasons for the virtual trebling of the population of Upper Canada (or Canada West) between 1840–60, including an increase in the indigenous population, as settlers raised families.

In anticipation of the arrival of immigrants to Upper Canada, previously-defined counties were split into townships, before each township was subdivided into lots, usually of 50, 100 or 200 acres in size. Because southwestern Ontario was one of the most densely-forested regions, surveying was arduous and required the clearance of roads or trails for access. Once lots were defined, the government met the additional cost of building small log cabins or shanties for the temporary shelter of the settlers.

Compared to the earlier, more generous provision for Loyalists, the *Emigrants Handbook*, drafted in 1832 by A.C. Buchanan, the Crown's Chief Agent for the Superintendence of Settlers and Emigrants to Upper and Lower Canada, clearly indicated that no further help would be provided, stating that the Crown: '... will make no advances in provisions or utensils, and settlers must depend entirely upon their own resources for bringing their lands into cultivation.' So, from the outset, starting in the immediate vicinity of their crude log cabins or shanties, settlers were expected to clear the surrounding forest and bush in order to provide fuel and create plots in which to cultivate the food and fodder on which survival through the first harsh Canadian winter would depend. It has been estimated that, in a good year, a settler might have cleared 4 acres around tree stumps that were left to rot in the ground, but most clearance was achieved at a slower rate. Thus the time and effort needed to develop a viable farm would have been considerable, although the felling and sale of timber, mainly a winter occupation, was a secondary source of income while land was being cleared.

The area north of the Thames River, including Mosa Township, was surveyed in readiness for settlement between 1814–25. Mosa itself was surveyed in 1820, and the first settlers moved there soon after. By the most curious of coincidences, the surveyor's name was Burwell – Lt Col Mahlon Burwell. It is a measure of his lasting contribution to the shaping of the Canadian landscape that the imprint of the roads and lots he mapped out, including the lots close to Newbury on which my forebears settled, is still clearly evident in satellite images.

At first, the settlement of Mosa proceeded at a comparatively slow pace. A survey conducted in 1825 estimated that the neighbouring townships of Mosa, Ekfrid and Caradoc had a combined population of 274. In 1830, it was reported that Mosa's population was 276. In the early 1840s, William Henry Smith surveyed the state of development in Upper Canada's burgeoning townships. His *Gazetteer*, published in 1846, records that Mosa's population was 1,154 in 1842 and that 25,243 acres had been taken up, one-fifth of which was under cultivation.

The next estimate of the township's population was provided by an anonymously-written *History of the County of Middlesex* which reported a figure of 1,775 inhabitants in 1850. A decade later, the 1861 census recorded a population of 3,030, inclusive of the villages of Wardsville (named after the first man to settle) and Newbury. Both Wardsville, which was a hamlet with only twelve buildings in 1840, and Newbury, where the first house was built in 1850, increased in size and diversity during this period, each growing to populations of around 500 by 1860, and with each community having two or three hotels, a post office, numerous stores and tradesmen's business premises. For Newbury in particular, the main stimulus for its development was the opening of a mainline station on the Great Western Railway in 1854, the year in which it became fully operational along its entire route from Niagara Falls to Windsor. By that date, the settlers had also begun to consolidate their position, with the late 1840s and the following decade marked by the building of churches for different denominational groups, the opening of schools and the inauguration of such organisations as the Orange Order and Masonic Lodges.

After 1861, the township's population continued to increase over the next decade with, for example, the population of Newbury reaching around 800 by the time of its formal incorporation as a village in 1872. However, it is likely that those were peak figures. A map of land holdings in Mosa Township drawn in the late 1870s shows that all except about twenty lots had been occupied, with the remainder still in the hands of the Canada Company, which had assumed responsibility for the sale of Crown lands in 1824. The untaken lots were mostly in, or adjacent to, the area now covered by the Big Bend Conservation Area, so it would seem that area was never cleared for cultivation.

After its arrival in Mosa, the railroad network continued to expand, opening up for development the prairie provinces of Manitoba, Saskatchewan and Alberta, and eventually providing a transcontinental link to British Columbia. In addition to attracting new settlers, that expansion encouraged some of those who were already settled to move west. My great great grandparents, Cornelius and Rebecca (Turner) Babcock, resettled in Manitoba as part of that population shift.

The effects of population decrease in areas left behind were evident in the 1901 census of Mosa Township, which recorded a population of 2,673 persons, inclusive of 457 who were then living in Newbury. Over a century later, in 2006, the village's website reported a population of 408. Canada's continuing economic development, including the exploitation of Alberta's oil sand deposits, is now a stimulus for the migration of younger generations. In years to come, once-thriving communities like Newbury may be obliged to confront a further decrease in population as younger people move on, leaving behind an increasingly higher proportion of older residents.

This was the rapidly-developing new nation that my forebears chose as their home. The accompanying family tree introduces my father's family in direct lines of descent from the late eighteenth century onwards.

FAMILY TREE

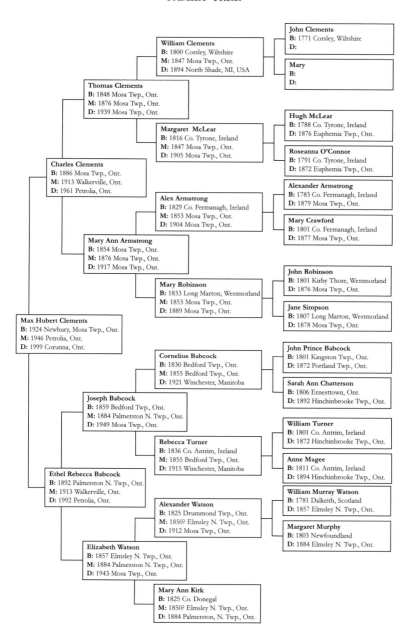

John Clements
B: 1771 Corsley, Wiltshire
D:

Mary
B:
D:

William Clements
B: 1800 Corsley, Wiltshire
M: 1847 Mosa Twp., Ont.
D: 1894 North Shade, MI, USA

Thomas Clements
B: 1848 Mosa Twp., Ont.
M: 1876 Mosa Twp., Ont.
D: 1939 Mosa Twp., Ont.

Hugh McLear
B: 1788 Co. Tyrone, Ireland
D: 1876 Euphemia Twp., Ont.

Roseanna O'Connor
B: 1791 Co. Tyrone, Ireland
D: 1872 Euphemia Twp., Ont.

Margaret McLear
B: 1816 Co. Tyrone, Ireland
M: 1847 Mosa Twp., Ont.
D: 1905 Mosa Twp., Ont.

Charles Clements
B: 1886 Mosa Twp., Ont.
M: 1913 Walkerville, Ont.
D: 1961 Petrolia, Ont.

Alexander Armstrong
B: 1783 Co. Fermanagh, Ireland
D: 1879 Mosa Twp., Ont.

Mary Crawford
B: 1801 Co. Fermanagh, Ireland
D: 1877 Mosa Twp., Ont.

Alex Armstrong
B: 1829 Co. Fermanagh, Ireland
M: 1853 Mosa Twp., Ont.
D: 1904 Mosa Twp., Ont.

Mary Ann Armstrong
B: 1854 Mosa Twp., Ont.
M: 1876 Mosa Twp., Ont.
D: 1917 Mosa Twp., Ont.

John Robinson
B: 1801 Kirby Thore, Westmorland
D: 1876 Mosa Twp., Ont.

Jane Simpson
B: 1807 Long Marton, Westmorland
D: 1878 Mosa Twp., Ont.

Mary Robinson
B: 1833 Long Marton, Westmorland
M: 1853 Mosa Twp., Ont.
D: 1889 Mosa Twp., Ont.

Max Hubert Clements
B: 1924 Newbury, Mosa Twp., Ont.
M: 1946 Petrolia, Ont.
D: 1999 Corunna, Ont.

John Prince Babcock
B: 1801 Kingston Twp., Ont.
D: 1872 Portland Twp., Ont.

Sarah Ann Chatterson
B: 1806 Ernesttown, Ont.
D: 1892 Hinchinbrooke Twp., Ont.

Cornelius Babcock
B: 1830 Bedford Twp., Ont.
M: 1855 Bedford Twp., Ont.
D: 1921 Winchester, Manitoba

Joseph Babcock
B: 1859 Bedford Twp., Ont.
M: 1884 Palmerston N. Twp., Ont.
D: 1949 Mosa Twp., Ont.

William Turner
B: 1801 Co. Antrim, Ireland
D: 1872 Hinchinbrooke Twp., Ont.

Anne Magee
B: 1811 Co. Antrim, Ireland
D: 1894 Hinchinbrooke Twp., Ont.

Rebecca Turner
B: 1836 Co. Antrim, Ireland
M: 1855 Bedford Twp., Ont.
D: 1915 Winchester, Manitoba

Ethel Rebecca Babcock
B: 1892 Palmerston N. Twp., Ont.
M: 1913 Walkerville, Ont.
D: 1992 Petrolia, Ont.

William Murray Watson
B: 1781 Dalkeith, Scotland
D: 1857 Elmsley N. Twp., Ont.

Margaret Murphy
B: 1803 Newfoundland
D: 1884 Elmsley N. Twp., Ont.

Alexander Watson
B: 1825 Drummond Twp., Ont.
M: 1850? Elmsley N. Twp., Ont.
D: 1912 Mosa Twp., Ont.

Elizabeth Watson
B: 1857 Elmsley N. Twp., Ont.
M: 1884 Palmerston N. Twp., Ont.
D: 1943 Mosa Twp., Ont.

Mary Ann Kirk
B: 1825 Co. Donegal
M: 1850? Elmsley N. Twp., Ont.
D: 1884 Palmerston, N. Twp., Ont.

4

Puritans and Loyalists

In the truest sense, my paternal ancestors were pioneers. With the exceptions of the Turner and McLear families, who left their homes in County Antrim and County Tyrone in the late 1840s, they made their transatlantic crossings before the Act of Union, 1841 (the first building block in Canada's federal structure), and in advance of the mass emigration from Europe after the mid-century failures of the potato crop. In the case of some families, including the Babcocks, the crossing was made even earlier, just a few years after the Pilgrim Fathers' epic voyage aboard the *Mayflower* in 1620.

Generally, those forebears who arrived in Upper Canada settled on plots of virgin forest and bush, from which clearings were made and marshland drained to create fields in which to sow their first crops and grow fodder for their beasts. To supplement that precarious living, they hewed timber, some for their own consumption, some for public works and some for export, and were also likely to have helped with the building of roads. If life was challenging for the men, it must have been the more so for their womenfolk. They had to create homes out of log shanties and other crude dwellings lacking basic amenities of any kind. In most cases, they were also obliged to deal with one pregnancy after another while simultaneously caring for their large families, coping with death and disease, and undertaking their share of the work involved in cultivating kitchen gardens and animal husbandry. *Roughing it in the Bush,* Susannah Moodie's choice of title for the widely-acclaimed account of her own experience of settling in Canada, could not have been more apt.

After the Seven Years War (1756–63), remembered most for General James Wolfe's victory over the French at Quebec City in 1759, which enabled Britain to gain control over the territories of New France, the early stages of Canada's evolution into nationhood were shaped by two other conflicts. The first was the American War of Independence (1776–83), which marked the loss of thirteen former British colonies and the formation of the United States. The second was the war of 1812–14 in which an attempt by the United States to extend its hegemony over other parts of North America that were still under British Crown control was successfully resisted. As ancestors on my paternal grandmother's side took part in both of the latter conflicts, they provide a family link to significant events associated with Canada's origins. And since her North American roots are the deepest, the following account of my paternal ancestry takes her family's story as its starting point.

The first of my forebears to set foot on Canadian soil was my great great great great grandfather, Benjamin Babcock. He was a United Empire Loyalist who fought on the side of the British Crown during the American War of Independence. However, he was not the first member of the family to set foot on the North American continent. Records show that the first to make that transatlantic voyage did so as part of an exodus of English Puritans, the Great Migration, who forsook their homeland between 1630–42. Following the decision of King Charles I to dissolve parliament in 1629 and contemporaneous measures to suppress non-conformist religious belief, introduced by William Laud in his roles first as Bishop of London and then as Archbishop of Canterbury, that exodus took them to the Massachusetts Bay and Plymouth colonies in a quest for religious and political freedom. Ultimately, those actions by Charles I and his archbishop were to precipitate the king's execution and the English Civil War. In an uninterrupted patrilineal line of descent to 1892, when my paternal grandmother was born, James Babcock, going back eleven generations, was amongst those who sought the perceived freedoms of the New World.

James and Sarah (Brown) Babcock

Other than his date of birth in 1612, and the indication that his surname was originally Badcock (the alternative spelling was used by later generations after his death) little is known about James Babcock's origins. The current consensus is that James, the known progenitor of the North American Babcock family, most probably made his transatlantic crossing in the latter half of the period spanned by the Great Migration.

James Babcock's name first appeared in North American records in 1642, when he was admitted as an inhabitant of Portsmouth, Rhode Island. By then, he had married Sarah Brown, who had already given birth to their first child, James, in Portsmouth one year earlier, suggesting he had been in North America for some time. His presence in Portsmouth would further suggest that, after his arrival in the Massachusetts Bay colony, he found common cause with others who were opposed to the theocratic yoke imposed by the elders of that colony, and whose opposition had resulted in banishment or voluntary onward migration.

Most notably, the latter included the Quaker, Roger Williams, who founded the Providence Plantations in 1636. Others included William Coddington, a Boston merchant who is said to have purchased Aquidneck (now the island of Rhode Island) from Narragansett Sachems for forty fathoms of white beads, ten coats and twenty hoes; Anne and William Hutchinson and their followers, who settled in Pocasset (later re-named Portsmouth) on that island in 1638; and others who established another settlement at Newport in the south of the island in 1639.

James Babcock's name did not appear among the signatories to the Portsmouth Compact (sometimes also known as 'The Bodie Politicke'), which set out the principles in accordance with which the Pocasset settlement would be governed. Nevertheless, in 1643, a year after he was admitted as an inhabitant of Portsmouth, he was allocated 10 acres of land and, as a blacksmith, ordered to repair all arms. James and Sarah made Portsmouth their home for the next twenty years, during which three more children were born – John, from whom I am descended through ten generations, Job and Mary. James became increasingly involved in civic affairs, particularly following his admission as a Freeman in 1648. He held a succession of different offices, including appointment to the General Council in 1657. He was responsible for road building and also called upon to act as a mediator in land holding and boundary disputes, services for which he was rewarded with additional land grants.

The respect gained in the performance of those duties may account for James' recruitment to a Newport-based company, which purchased a tract of land previously occupied by Pequot First Nation people. Covering an area of approximately 200 square miles and located alongside the Pawcatuck River, the land was known as Misquamicut. It was a contentious purchase since ownership was also claimed by the Massachusetts Bay colony, and because some of the land was the subject of a hotly-disputed boundary between the Connecticut and Rhode Island colonies that continued long into the future.

To secure the purchase, James and his son John were appointed in 1661 to join an eighteen-strong party of Misquamicut Company members who were sent to survey the land and set out the boundaries of a new settlement, to be known as Westerly. Westerly was settled the following year, when James and his family were among its founder residents. Reflecting his status within the community, James was one of a group of five men who were made responsible for managing Westerly's civic affairs. His land holdings in Portsmouth were sold in 1665. Clearly, relocation to the new settlement was intended to be permanent.

Apart from a temporary strategic retreat to Aquidneck, which most of Westerly's inhabitants felt obliged to make to ensure their safety during the First Nation uprising known as King Philip's War (1675–76), James spent the remainder of his life in Westerly. At its incorporation in 1669, he was made a Freeman. He had 'earned his spurs' in part by his leadership in boundary disputes with the Connecticut colonists, both sides having attempted to extend their territory by encroaching claims on land adjacent to each other's riverside land holdings.

During the 1670s, theological imperatives led James and his family to shift their religious affiliation to the First Seventh Day Baptist Church, into which they were baptised in 1678. This new church had been established in 1671, when its founding members severed their connection with the First Baptist Church of Newport, itself an offshoot of an earlier schism in the Portsmouth Church.

James and Sarah's youngest son, Job, had already married Jane, a daughter of Sabbatarian elder John Crandall, in 1669. By that date, Sarah had passed away, most probably in 1665, and James had married Elizabeth March, with whom he had three more children. James died in Stonington in June 1679. He was interred in the Babcock family burial ground in Westerly.

Regrettably, the early Westerly settlers did not bequeath a contemporaneous account of their surroundings and experience. A history of Westerly written at a later date by the Rev Frederic Denison, a descendant of one of the earliest settlers, envisaged his forebears' circumstances as follows:

> Only those who have travelled in a wild, unsubdued country can form any proximate idea of the appearance and condition of this region when it was first entered by the colonists. And only those who have experienced pioneer life are able to conceive the trials and hardships endured by the first settlers. As the region was naturally rough, the soil thin and stony, the forests dense and old, there being no rich, inviting river valley, nor any broad, commodious harbor, and all the country being still encompassed by remnants of savage tribes, while the wilderness was the full haunt of ravenous beasts, its settlement by whites was inevitably slow and difficult.

John and Mary (Lawton) Babcock

John Babcock, my antecedent going back ten generations, was born in Portsmouth in 1644. In or around 1662, he married Mary, the daughter of George and Elizabeth (Hazard) Lawton. Like James Babcock, both her father and maternal grandfather, Thomas Hazard, had crossed the Atlantic during the Great Migration. George Lawton, originally from Cranfield, Bedfordshire, became one of Portsmouth's most prominent citizens.

Around one year before his marriage, when only seventeen years old, John Babcock was one of the party of eighteen people (together with his father) who were appointed to survey the Misquamicut Company's purchase. He was also a member of the group who occupied the land for a period during the summer of 1661 to establish a claim to its ownership. Accordingly, he was allocated one of the surveyed lots, and at the incorporation of Westerly was admitted as a Freeman alongside his father and brothers James (junior) and Job. Later, in 1771, in response to the Rhode Island colony's concern about the allegiance of those who had settled on its western boundary with Connecticut, all four were listed amongst the inhabitants who formally affirmed their continuing loyalty to the Crown and the colony.

However, other events demonstrated that John's loyalties could be governed by more pragmatic considerations. During King Philip's War, when other Westerly settlers beat a strategic retreat to the perceived fastness of Aquidneck, John and his family remained in Westerly – if not as the only family to do so, then as part of a very small minority who opted to stay close to home. To protect his interests, John sided with Connecticut. He is said to have volunteered for the Stonington Militia, and to have taken part in the Great Swamp Fight in the vicinity of Kingston in December 1675. He is also said to have been admitted as a Freeman of Connecticut in 1676 and, after the war, to have been awarded bounty land in Voluntown, to the north of Stonington.

But John Babcock's attachment to Rhode Island did not end

there. In 1678, he was elected by the General Court of Rhode Island to the post of Conservator of the Peace in Westerly. And three months after his father's death the following year, alongside thirty-two other Westerly residents, he swore a new oath of allegiance to the Crown and the colony of Rhode Island. He then served as Westerly's Deputy to the Colonial Legislature in 1682 and 1684, and most probably would have rendered even greater public service but for his early death in his forty-first year in 1685, only six years after his father's demise. His bones were laid to rest alongside his father's in Westerly.

John and Mary (Lawton) Babcock had ten children – I am descended from Job, the fifth to be born. The youngest, Oliver, who later sold his father's bounty land in Voluntown, was only two years old when his father died. Mary faced widowhood with a young family, although she did remarry in 1698. She passed away in 1711.

John Babcock died intestate. So it became the responsibility of the Westerly Town Council to make an inventory of his possessions and draw up a will. In that will, to which Mary was made executrix, the oldest son, James, inherited all of his father's landed property, but conveyed one-half to his mother. Other possessions, valued at £790.3s. (said to be one of the largest estates at that time), were divided between the widow, who received one third, and the other children, who shared the remainder. The inventory makes interesting reading. Apart from its listing of livestock, household furnishings and equipment, farm implements, weaponry, and 'Three canooes and three padles', it listed 'one negger boy' and 'two Injin men and Indian garls'. As many of the First Nation people on the losing side in King Philip's War were forced into slavery, either in the North American colonies or overseas, the possibility that the latter 'possessions' were also slaves cannot be overlooked.

Job and Deborah (Reynolds) Babcock

These are my forebears going back nine generations. Job, the first in a line of three ancestors of that name, was born in Westerly in 1671. His wife, Deborah, was born four years later. Her paternal grandparents and great grandparents, originally from Glastonbury, Somerset, had settled in Weymouth, Massachusetts after taking part in the Great Migration.

Job and Deborah were married in 1695 and raised a family of six, three sons and three daughters – I am descended from the oldest son, who was named after his father. Job and Deborah Babcock did not stay in Westerly. By 1723, they were residents of South Kingston, where Job and five other men were elected that year to form the community's first town council. Job followed the family tradition of public service. For example, in 1727, he was both selected as South Kingston's Deputy to the General Court of Rhode Island and appointed as Protonotary. It would appear that he had sufficient land to have conveyed part of those holdings to his sons in 1731. Job passed away in South Kingston 1755, around one year after Deborah's demise.

Job and Elizabeth (Hull) Babcock

The second Job was born in 1697. In 1717, he married Elizabeth, who was born in Kingston in 1700. Her great great grandparents and great grandparents had also participated in the Great Migration. In almost every case, they found the intolerance of their religious beliefs in the Massachusetts Bay and Plymouth colonies in which they first settled unbearable, in some instances resulting in banishment and in others voluntary onward migration to Rhode Island, where they were to find greater freedom to express and exercise their faith. Thus it was that Elizabeth's great grandfather William Dyer became one of those who signed the Portsmouth Compact in 1638. His wife, Mary (Barrett) Dyer, also left her mark on the pages of history, but in more tragic circumstances. She is now remembered as a martyr who, on the orders of Governor Endicott, suffered death by hanging in Boston in 1660 after refusing to recant her Quaker faith. Depictions of her final walk to the scaffold show her surrounded by drummers who, acting on the governor's orders, were beating their drums to 'drown out' any last words she might have wished to address to the crowd of onlookers.

After their marriage in Kingston, Job and Elizabeth Babcock set up home in South Kingston, where they had a family of five; two sons, (I am descended from the youngest) and three daughters. Records indicate that Job died in 1775, four years after his wife's death in 1771.

Job and Susannah (Hopkins) Babcock

The third Job was born in South Kingston in 1722. His marriage to Susannah Hopkins in November 1748 was also celebrated in South Kingston. However, by the time the first of their sons, David, was born in 1752, they had relocated to Haverstraw, Orange County, on the west bank of the Hudson River, around 30 miles north of New York City. Benjamin, their second son, was born there in 1754. Susannah died in 1760, her husband fifteen years later, on the eve of the American Revolution. It was from their family home in Orange County in the State of New York that David and Benjamin enlisted in the British Crown's cause.

Benjamin and Rachel (Decker) Babcock

Benjamin Babcock, my great great great great grandfather, was a United Empire Loyalist. That title was a badge of honour conferred upon those whose loyalty led them to fight for the British Crown during the American War of Independence, and who were relocated to the British North American territories, the nucleus of modern

Canada, after the defeat of George III's forces. While probably sympathetic with demands for better governance of the colonies set out in a Declaration of Rights in 1775, United Empire Loyalists did not subscribe to the subsequent Declaration of Independence on 4 July 1776, which precipitated the war. They paid a very heavy price for their allegiance, suffering disgrace, confiscation of land and other property and, for many, banishment.

Historians estimate that around 100,000 fled the newly-formed United States. Some returned to Europe or resettled in the West Indies. Others, the United Empire Loyalists, migrated to what remained of British North America. Around 10,000 to 12,000 travelled to the Bay of Quinté, where five new townships, including Kingston and Ernesttown, were hastily surveyed in readiness for their occupation. Another 25,000 to 30,000 travelled by sea to resettle in Nova Scotia, New Brunswick and the St Lawrence River valley.

In acknowledgement of the United Empire Loyalists' service, the Crown awarded grants of land and supplied provisions and agricultural implements. In 1789, in further acknowledgement of loyalists' support and sacrifice, their children were also granted entitlement to land grants of 200 acres each to sons on reaching the age of 21 years and daughters on reaching that age or, if sooner, on marriage. In return for this generosity, the United Empire Loyalists and their families were expected to provide the nucleus of a militia in the event of future conflict with the United States.

Benjamin Babcock is believed to have served as a private in the Loyal American Regiment, formed in 1777 by Beverly Robinson, a childhood friend of George Washington and reputedly one of New York's wealthiest landowners. Although there is no record of Benjamin's experience of the war, it is known that his brother David achieved the rank of captain and participated in reconnaissance and intelligence-gathering operations under the command of Col Henry Johnson. The two brothers appear to have ended the war together under siege at Major Ward's block house on Long Island.

After the war, in 1786, in response to the appointment of

commissioners who were charged by act of parliament to head an enquiry into the 'Losses and Sufferings of the American Loyalists', David petitioned the Crown for the reimbursement of expenditure he had incurred on the erection of a block house at Slongo and a fort and block house at Bergen Neck; the loss of cordwood, two horses and a wagon taken by 'rebel' forces during an assault on Bergen Neck; and loss of pay during his command of that fortified stronghold. The claim amounted to £315.9s.4d.

At the end of the war in 1783, Benjamin and David Babcock had sailed from New York to the Maritime colonies. The former was a bachelor and the latter was accompanied by his first wife, Thankful Barbara (née Garlick). Their presence there is marked by Benjamin's inclusion in the 'Muster Roll of Disbanded Officers Discharged and Disbanded Soldiers and Loyalists taken in the County of Annapolis betwixt the 18th and 24th of June, 1784', and David's award of a land grant in Tusket River, Nova Scotia. But they did not put down permanent roots. After the tragic death of David's wife in a house fire in 1789, they decided to join other United Empire Loyalists who had settled in the townships developed for loyalist occupation on the Bay of Quinté.

Soon after that relocation, Benjamin Babcock met Rachel Decker. They were married in 1789 and settled in Kingston, where the first of their children was born the following year. Apart from her birth in 1769 and indications that she was most probably of German descent and was a resident of Ernesttown before her marriage, little else is known about Rachel Decker. However, those roots appear to have spawned a household in which the German language was spoken and, in the longer term, an Anglo-German dynasty, many of whose members down to her great great granddaughter Ethel (my paternal grandmother) reported their 'tribal' origin as 'German' in censuses to 1911, as well as in other official records. The name Pamina, given to two of Benjamin and Rachel's daughters, the first of whom died in infancy, is German and might also have been Rachel's mother's name. At the time, a Hanoverian king was on the British throne and German mercenaries had been drafted in to bolster the Crown's forces during the War of Independence. Anglo-German alliances and marriages were less exceptional than they were to become after France became Britain's ally in other conflicts that followed the unification of Germany under Otto von Bismarck.

In 1792, the year after the separate colonies of Upper and Lower Canada were created by the Constitutional Act, Benjamin Babcock was granted a lot of 200 acres in Kingston. He was still living there in 1803, when his daughter Elizabeth, the eighth child, was born. However, by 1809, Benjamin and his family had moved to Ernesttown, the recorded birthplace of his four youngest children. Benjamin Babcock died in Ernesttown in August, 1829, aged seventy-five years. A record of his wife Rachel's death has not been traced.

Babcock family historians have reviewed the land grant petitions made by Benjamin and Rachel's children. Those sources, which incidentally confirm both Benjamin's United Empire Loyalist status and his children's identities, show that most of the children were granted land either in Camden Township in Addington County or the townships of Portland and Bedford in Frontenac County. The same records indicate that one daughter, Elizabeth, was described as a 'lunatic' in the petition my great great great grandfather, John Prince Babcock, presented on her behalf in 1838.

John Prince and Sarah Ann (Chatterson) Babcock

John Prince Babcock was born in Kingston in 1801, the seventh of his parents' twelve children. In 1824, he married Sarah Ann Chatterson (b. 1806), a young woman of Dutch-American descent. When their first child, William, was born in 1828, they were residents of Colebrook, a small settlement to the south of Varty Lake in Camden Township. John Prince's petition for a land grant as a son of a United Empire Loyalist was not made until 1834. Meanwhile, the family had moved to Bedford Township, where their second child, Cornelius (my great great grandfather), was born in 1830. John

Prince and Sarah Ann continued to farm in Bedford until 1848. Six more children were born there between 1833–45. Their youngest child, Charles (b. 1849), though, was born in Verona, Portland Township.

John Prince Babcock was still farming in the vicinity of Verona at the time of the 1871 Federal Census. He died there the following year, aged seventy-one years. Sarah Ann outlived her husband by another twenty years, passing away in Oak Flats, Hinchinbrooke Township in 1892 at the age of eighty-six. In Hinchinbrooke, Sarah Ann would have been close to most of her children, who had obtained land in the township, where their presence as farmers was recorded in censuses to 1911.

Cornelius and Rebecca (Turner) Babcock

Cornelius Babcock was born in Bedford Township in October 1830. He married Rebecca Turner in September 1855. Rebecca, born in County Antrim in January 1836, was the daughter of William and Ann (Magee) Turner. He was Anglican, his wife a Roman Catholic. Rebecca arrived in Canada West in 1847, having made the transatlantic crossing with her parents and four siblings in their bid to escape the disastrous effects of famine in their native Ireland.

After their marriage, Cornelius and Rebecca moved onto their own lot in Bedford Township. They were there in 1861, with a young family of two, Lizzie aged four years and Joseph, my great grandfather, aged two. Their first-born son, William, had died in infancy. They were still in Bedford ten years later, their family having increased by five more children. By 1881, however, with yet another three young mouths to feed, they had relocated to Clarendon and Miller Township. During the next decade, many of the older children married, leaving Cornelius and Rebecca at home with only the four youngest, their ages ranging from fifteen to twenty-two years.

The last quarter of the nineteenth century witnessed the 'colonisation' of Canada's prairies. In the mid-to-late 1890s, spearheaded by Edward Babcock, the eighth of Cornelius and Rebecca's eleven children, his parents and some of his siblings joined that westward migration. In their case, the destination was the region between the Red and Assiniboia rivers in Manitoba, the location of the Métis rebellion that Louis Riel fomented in 1869–70. It was there, a quarter of a century later, that Edward met his wife, Isabella Hudson, who he married in Morton on New Year's Day, 1896, and where his parents and some of his siblings were later to join him. When the 1901 census was taken, Cornelius was already present in his son's home in Winchester, near Souris. Since Rebecca's presence was not recorded, it is presumed she was elsewhere, in the home of one of her other children.

However, both Cornelius and Rebecca were living as near neighbours to Edward's family in 1911. By that time, Edward and Isabella had nine children to care for, of whom, sadly, three were subsequently lost to a diphtheria epidemic. When she died in 1915, aged seventy-nine years, Rebecca still was living in Winchester. Cornelius also ended his days there. He passed away in June 1921, in his ninety-first year. His obituary in *The Deloraine Times* (6 August 1921) confirmed his last years had been spent in close proximity to many of his children and grandchildren.

5

A Scottish Soldier

Before embarking on this quest, I was not aware of any ancestral ties with Scotland, my home for the previous quarter century. So the discovery that my paternal grandmother came from Scottish roots was quite a surprise. Tracing those roots proved to be one of the more challenging lines of enquiry, but all the more intriguing and rewarding when I eventually found that the starting point of the trail traced back over time was within a few miles of my home.

The first indication was the finding that my paternal grandmother's own grandfather, Alexander Watson, had Scottish roots. From official records, the initial impression was that he had travelled to Canada in the late 1840s or early 1850s. Accordingly, the first efforts to trace him concentrated on Scottish records of people of that name whose births were registered in or around 1825, that year having been indicated by Canadian sources of a much later date. But those lines of enquiry were both frustrating and ultimately abortive, not least because most of the numerous 'Alexander Watsons' who were fifteen to seventeen years old when the 1841 census was recorded had already left their family homes to live in other households as apprentices, lodgers or servants. It seemed that prospects of tracing Alexander Watson's forebears were exceedingly slim. Months later, there was a breakthrough when a speculative review of the Canada West 1851 census located the recently-married Alexander and his wife in North Elmsley Township, Lanark County, Ontario. The same source indicated that he had not been born in Scotland, but in the neighbouring township, Drummond.

In turn, that information led to the identification of his father, my great great great grandfather William Watson, who had also moved to North Elmsley after an earlier period of residence in Drummond Township. The 1851 census recorded William Watson's place and date of birth as 'Edinburgh' in or around 1782. Scottish records showed that several 'William Watsons' were registered in Edinburgh and the Lothians at about that time. It was possible to exclude some from further consideration because they could still be traced as living in Scotland after 1820, when Canadian sources indicated that William Watson was already in Drummond Township. Nevertheless, once again the trail was blocked, and remained so until the very helpful assistance of a Lanark, Ontario-based family research agency resulted in the unearthing of William Watson's land grant and military records. It was the latter source that confirmed he had actually been born in Dalkeith, the county town of Midlothian, just 3 miles from my home.

William and Margaret (Murphy) Watson

Scottish records indicate that William Murray Watson was born in Dalkeith on 3 August 1781. He was the second of four children born to Alexander and Marion (Murray) Watson, who were married in Dalkeith in April 1779.

William's mother, Marion, was born in May 1759 in the Berwickshire parish of Channelkirk at Hartside, a small, isolated farmstead on the southern slopes of the Moorfoot Hills. From the registration of Marion's baptism, in which there was no reference to a father, it seems her mother, who bore the same name and who was born in 1728, was a single parent.

William's father, Alexander Watson, was born in Dalkeith in August 1758. He was the son of James and Mary (Briggs) Watson, who were born in 1721 and 1724 respectively, and who were married in Dalkeith in August 1749.

David Macbeth Moir's novel *The Life of Mansie Wauch Tailor in Dalkeith* provides a contemporaneous description of the town into which William Watson was born and the local merchant and trades community amongst whom he spent his early years. Throughout the eighteenth century, from their palace on the edge of the town, the Dukes of Buccleuch had dominated its civic and business affairs. In 1801, Dalkeith had a population of 3,906, around one-third of its present size. It lies 6 miles southeast of Edinburgh, for which in recent times it has increasingly served as a dormitory suburb. But that has not always been so. As the county town of Midlothian, it has also had its own distinct identity as a market for the surrounding agricultural and market gardening community, and as the centre of a coal mining industry dating back to the thirteenth century when Cistercian monks from Newbattle Abbey were the first to exploit local coal reserves.

Records indicate that William Watson's great grandfather Alexander Briggs, his grandfather James Watson, and his father Alexander Watson were all local merchants, suggesting that the family were members of the town's business community. Such membership is certainly suggested by entries in the town's registers of marriages and births. Thus, when William's parents, Alexander and Marion, formally announced their intention to marry, one cautioner (sponsor or adviser) was a local surgeon. At William's baptism, the two official witnesses were Robert Brunton, clock and watchmaker, and David Hutcheson, proprietor of the town's iron mill and member of the board of twelve trustees (which also included the Duke of Buccleuch) responsible for the town's governance.

David Hutcheson's son, also named David, was one of William Watson's contemporaries, which may have resulted in the older Hutcheson taking William on as an apprentice at the iron mill to train as an ironsmith, the occupation noted in later records. While some records of the affairs of Dalkeith's Incorporation of Hammermen (the town's guild of metal working trades) have survived, those relating to the period during which William would have served time as an apprentice or journeyman (c.1795–1803) have been lost. So there is no direct corroboration of the vocational training he received.

In 1803, William Watson turned his back on his job, family and the town in which he had been raised by enlisting as a soldier. While his personal reasons for that decision may never be known, historians have drawn attention to more general factors that could have influenced the recruitment at that time of Lowland Scots, who previously had not demonstrated the same inclination to enlist for military service as their Highland counterparts, even though the ongoing war with Napoleon's forces was resulting in the mobilisation of forces on an unprecedented scale.

In *Scotland's Empire 1600–1815*, Professor Tom Devine proposes three possible explanations for an increase in the number of Lowlanders who opted for military service around the time William Watson decided to enlist. First, there was a longstanding differential in wages, including those for craftsmen, in Scotland and England, with the Scots worse off. Second, the transformation of Scottish society associated with the emergence of a market economy – industrialisation, urbanisation and the need for increased efficiency in agriculture to provide for those no longer dependent on the land – was not achieved without significant unemployment and hardship. Third, the changes in land ownership associated with agricultural improvement, resulting in loss of tenancies and legal rights of ownership, created a class of non-inheriting children of not only farmers but also those in other occupations, for whom there was no effective safety net. As Poor Law provision could not meet all needs, the promise of regular pay and rations must have been a strong inducement to enlist.

For William Watson, ironsmith, it is possible that market forces in his own trade were also of particular significance. Local historians have found evidence that an iron foundry was built in Dalkeith in 1648. The source of that information was the record of a claim against the Buccleuch estate for non payment for jobs the ironworks proprietor carried out between 1738–51. That business, servicing local farms, coal mines and other industries, also appears to have been well established when Henry Kalmeter from Sweden visited the town in 1719 in the course of a survey of mining and associated trades around the Firth of Forth. His journal noted the presence of forge hammers in Dalkeith. The foundry is believed to have flourished throughout the eighteenth century, with David Hutcheson taking over proprietorship in 1761 from his uncle William Gray, who had pursued the Duke of Buccleuch for debt.

However, from the 1790s onward, the rapid expansion of iron-works at Carron, which had seventeen furnaces in operation in 1796, and elsewhere in Scotland's central industrial belt, marked the onset of significant competition that led eventually to the closure of Dalkeith's iron mill and its transformation into a corn mill soon after the older David Hutcheson's death in 1811. William Watson's decision to enlist could well have been made because he foresaw an inevitable loss of employment and associated economic insecurity.

Military records show that William Watson's army career began with his enlistment in the 26th Regiment of Foot, the 'Cameronians', on 15 August 1803, twelve days after his twenty-second birthday. Andrew Ross's history of the regiment (in *The Lowland Scots Regiments*, edited by Sir Herbert Maxwell) sets out some of the background. In May 1787, the regiment had been posted to Canada, to return in 1800. In 1801, it formed part of an expeditionary force under Sir Ralph Abercrombie that was posted to Egypt, where it was involved in an eventually successful siege of Alexandria. However, that posting exacted a significant toll in dysentery and ophthalmia that depleted its ranks before the regiment embarked on its homeward passage in October 1802. From November 1802 to February 1803, the regiment was stationed in Stirling, before a further posting to Fort George near Ardesier on the Moray Firth. On the last day of July 1803, it sailed south to Leith, before resuming its station at Falkirk and Stirling. At that juncture, under the Additional Forces Act, 1803, a second battalion was raised. It would appear that William Watson's enlistment was in response to that recruitment drive. Thomas Carter's history of the regiment records that, around the time of his enlistment: 'Upwards of one thousand men, raised under the act in Scotland, joined the Regiment at Stirling and Linlithgow in August and the second battalion, for which letters of service had been previously received, was then formed.' It was followed by an early posting to Ireland.

William Watson's commitment to military service seems to have been uncertain, marked by a series of short-term or limited engagements rather than a longer-term commitment. His service record indicates that he was one of a large contingent from his battalion who resisted efforts to persuade them to transfer into the 1st Battalion in readiness for its involvement in a campaign in northwest Europe. Though possibly not the most courageous decision, it may have been a wise one, for many of the officers and other ranks from the 1st Batallion lost their lives when storms in the North Sea in November 1805 caused the sinking of the *Maria* and the *Aurora*, two of the ships that were deployed for transport to Germany.

In the event, William Watson continued to serve in the 2nd Battalion until December 1806 when, following a merger with other limited service personnel from the 2nd Battalion of the 42nd Highlanders, the 5th Garrison Battalion was formed in Dublin. He was not called upon to see action in the ongoing conflict with Napoleon's forces, but remained in Ireland. It was there in Dublin, on 30 August 1808, that William Watson transferred into the 103rd Regiment of Foot. The record of that transfer is of interest both in confirming that he signed on for another limited engagement and in providing details of his birthplace and occupation, as well as his personal features. The latter describe him as being five feet seven inches tall, of dark complexion, with a long face, brown hair and grey eyes.

William Watson continued to serve in Ireland until 1812, when, in response to United States aggression, his regiment was posted to Canada to assist in the defence of British North American interests. The 103rd was initially stationed in Newfoundland and then at Prescott, presumably to reinforce the loyalist militias of the Maritime territories in the event of a seaborne advance from the United States via the St Lawrence River. The regiment remained in those locations throughout 1813 and was not called upon to participate in any significant action until the following year.

However, during the closing phase of the 1812–14 war, the regiment, then numbering in total around 650 including officers and other ranks, was involved in two hard-fought, bloody actions on the Niagara frontier. They were the Battle of Lundy's Lane, a few miles west of the Niagara Falls, on 25 July 1814 and the month-long siege of Fort Erie, which started on 13 August 1814. In the latter action, the regiment lost not only its commanding officer but also over one-third of its men.

After the war, William Watson continued to serve as a private until his discharge from military service in Quebec in June 1816. While some members of his regiment returned to England, where it was disbanded at Chelmsford in 1817, he opted to remain in Upper Canada, undoubtedly attracted by the prospect of successfully petitioning for a land grant in acknowledgement of his service to the Crown. In 1819, he was granted 100 acres in Drummond Township in the Rideau Military Settlement, Perth. It was a Free Grant awarded for military service. Censuses of Drummond Township taken in 1820 and 1822 recorded his presence there as a single occupant. Other records indicate that between those dates, in September 1821, he was awarded a military pension.

On 10 December 1822, William, then aged forty-one, married Margaret Murphy who was just sixteen years old. There is little on record about the bride's origins except that the 1851 census recorded her birthplace as Newfoundland and that the record of her death gave Nova Scotia as her place of birth. Other sources suggest her parents were of Irish origin. Although the 1817, 1820 and 1822 censuses of Drummond and neighbouring townships record the presence there of Murphy families, no clear link has been identified. Family lore recalls how William Watson's marriage to a Roman Catholic resulted in the severance of ties with his Presbyterian family in Scotland, but it is not known whether that severance was occasioned by his marriage to Margaret Murphy or, taking age difference into account, an earlier marriage, possibly contracted during his prolonged period of military service in Ireland.

William and Margaret (Murphy) Watson's marriage ceremony was held at the First Presbyterian Church in Perth. The officiating clergyman was the Rev William Bell. He had been sent by the Associate Presbytery of Edinburgh to minister to assisted emigrants who had sailed from Greenock in 1815 and 1816, the original settlers of 'the Scotch Line' between Bathurst and North Burgess Townships, and also the Perth military settlement of discharged soldiers, who had started to arrive in the area around the same time. From his correspondence, it is apparent that the Rev Bell was also charged with the duty of conducting associated missionary work in the surrounding territory. With his family, he had sailed from Leith aboard the *Rothiemurchus* in May 1817. His letters have provided an illuminating account of the hazards of the transatlantic crossing and onward travel thereafter, as well as the challenges and hardships of the settlement process. They were published as a substantial compendium of information for intending emigrants in Edinburgh in 1824, under the title *Hints to Emigrants in a Series of Letters from Upper Canada*.

The Watsons spent the early years of their marriage in Drummond Township and the first three of their children were born there. They were Alexander, my great great grandfather, in 1825, followed by Edward and John. However, in August 1833, William purchased 100 acres in the neighbouring township of North Elmsley for £56.5s.

The move to North Elmsley took place a year or so after the completion of the Rideau Canal link from Bytown (which later became part of the federal capital, Ottawa) to Kingston. That new communication link became a main thoroughfare for both goods and new immigrants who, unlike William Watson, the Rev William Bell and their contemporaries, were no longer obliged to negotiate the rapids and other hazards along the St Lawrence River.

William Henry Smith visited the township in 1842. His *Gazetteer* reported that it then had a population of 1,154, with 18,603 acres of land taken up, of which 3,891 were under cultivation. He observed: 'A fair proportion of the land in this township is of good quality, and there are some tolerable farms in it. Timber: pine intermixed with hardwood. There are one grist and two saw mills in the township.'

After settling in North Elmsley, William and Margaret had more children, two sons, William and James, and two daughters, Elizabeth and Mary. When the 1851 census was taken, all but one were still in the family home. The exception was Alexander, who had recently married and was living nearby. William was a farmer and his sons Edward and John were working as labourers. The associated agricultural census described the family home as a 'log dwelling'. It also described the state of development of the lot, reporting that 20 of the 100 acres were under cultivation, of which 10 were used for crops and 10 for pasture, with the other 80 acres still woodland. Of the arable land, 5 acres had been used to grow wheat.

William Watson continued to farm the lot for another four years until April 1855, when it was sold to his son Edward for £200. William was then in his seventy-fourth year. He died two and a half years later in September 1857. His widow, Margaret, remained titular head of the family and was recorded as such in the 1861 census. Edward and his younger siblings were all unmarried and remained with her. By 1871, Edward had married and the others had left home. Margaret continued to live in North Elmsley with Edward and his family until her death in February 1884.

Alexander and Mary Ann (Kirk) Watson

My great great grandfather Alexander was born in Drummond Township in November 1825. In 1851, he was married and living in North Elmsley with his wife Mary Ann in a 'log shanty' on or near Mary Ann's brother William Kirk's lot. Apart from the existence of another brother, Andrew, and the indication that Kirk family members had emigrated from County Donegal, where Mary Ann was born in 1825, her origins remain obscure. Thus, her parents are the only two out of my sixteen paternal great great great grandparents whose identities have not been established.

Alexander and Mary Ann (Kirk) Watson continued to live in North Elmsley for at least the next decade. It is not known if

Alexander managed to acquire his own lot there or continued in employment as a labourer. During those years, the first three of their children were born. They were William, followed by my great grandmother, Elizabeth, and Andrew (John Watson's great grandfather). Soon after, the family moved to Ompah in Palmerston North Township, where two more children were born, Edward and Margaret. The 1871 census recorded their presence there, with Alexander, described as a farmer, evidently having obtained his own lot. In 1881, Alexander, Mary Ann and the four younger children were still together as a family in the same township, William having married.

After a long illness, during which she was nursed by Elizabeth, who was obliged to defer her marriage, Mary Ann passed away in 1884, aged fifty-nine years. Her demise allowed Elizabeth to proceed with her marriage to Joseph Babcock. Consequently, when the next census was taken, only the two youngest children were in the family home with their sixty-five year old widowed father, who was still farming. However, at some point during the next decade, Alexander Watson retired. The 1901 census revealed he had moved into Joseph and Elizabeth Babcock's home, in which other residents included my paternal grandmother, who was then only eight years old.

During the first decade of the new century, possibly taking advantage of the availability of land in Lambton and Middlesex counties which had been vacated by farming families who were attracted by the promise of a new life in the prairie provinces, Joseph and Elizabeth Babcock and her brothers and their families decided to relocate. The family story is that the land they farmed in Palmerston North had been difficult to work, with 'too many stones'. After a brief stay in or near Becher, Sombra Township in Lambton County, which appears to have been unsuccessful, they moved to Mosa Township, where Joseph and Elizabeth and their children, accompanied by Alexander Watson, took over land in the vicinity of Newbury. Alexander Watson lived with his daughter and son-in-law until he passed away in 1912, aged eighty-six years.

Joseph and Elizabeth (Watson) Babcock

These are my great grandparents, the parents of my paternal grandmother, Ethel (Babcock) Clements. Joseph, the oldest of Cornelius and Rebecca (Turner) Babcock's six sons who survived childhood, was born in Bedford Township in April 1859. He accompanied his parents when they moved from Bedford to Clarendon and Miller Township in the 1870s. When in his early twenties, he obtained land in Plevna, close to lots farmed by his father and brother Ephraim. His bride-to-be, Elizabeth, daughter of Alexander and Mary Ann (Kirk) Watson, lived in the neighbouring township, Palmerston North, where they were married in September 1884.

During the next two decades, Joseph and Elizabeth Babcock lived in Palmerston North Township. Their six children were born there between 1886 and 1898; George Alexander, Emma Jane, Mary Alice, Ethel Rebecca (my grandmother), John Wesley and Lawrence Sylvester (Joe Babcock's father). They arrived in Mosa Township around 1903, having first spent about two years in Lambton County, where they failed to put down new roots. They remained in Mosa. Both were interred at Oakland Cemetery, to the east of Wardsville, Elizabeth, who is remembered as a woman who rarely smiled, in 1943, aged eighty-six years, and Joseph after passing away in his ninetieth year in 1949.

Their children were of the last generation to reach adulthood before the outbreak of war in 1914. By that time, the nature of farming had changed and it had become increasingly difficult to make a living, unless additional land was obtained. The alternatives were either to take on other employment to supplement farm income or leave farming altogether. Those choices were reflected in the lives of Joseph and Elizabeth's children. George was attracted to the motor industry in Detroit, where he worked as a tool and die maker. After her marriage to Arthur Kunkel, Mary Alice also moved to Michigan where her husband spent his working life as a barber, but she returned to Mosa after her husband's death, bringing his remains with her for re-interment. John Wesley, who remained in

Newbury, combined working as a barber with other employment as a carpenter. Lawrence combined part-time farming and a job with Union Gas. The other two daughters, Emma, who married Ernest Armstrong, and my grandmother, who married Charles Clements, carried on the farming tradition, albeit with mixed success.

6

Westmorland to Youpper Canidy

My father's maternal and paternal ancestors arrived in Canada for quite different reasons. On his mother's side, James Babcock and his contemporaries crossed the Atlantic in pursuit of freedom to express and exercise their religious and political beliefs, and Benjamin Babcock and William Watson found themselves in Canada as a result of their participation in wars fought to defend the British Crown's interest in its North American colonies. On his father's side, ancestors (whose transatlantic voyages were mostly made in the early- to mid-1830s) were essentially economic migrants. For William Clements, Alexander Armstrong and John Robinson and their families, the main reason for emigrating was a desire to escape the unemployment and grinding poverty that accompanied the agricultural and industrial revolutions and the aftermath of the Napoleonic War.

Such escape, though, was not simply gifted on arrival in Upper Canada. It required effort and will to overcome the hardship and privation which have been widely chronicled, perhaps most notably by Susannah Moodie, but also in more prosaic fragments of correspondence between the new immigrants and family members left behind in their respective homelands. The Warner Collection (a.k.a. the Simpson Letters) comprises a series of letters, written between 1833–70, that were posted to their parents by the sons and daughters of an English farming family who settled in Mosa. Since their authors include my great great great grandparents, John and Jane (Simpson) Robinson, those letters provide a family-linked narrative of pioneers' experience of emigration and settlement.

John and Jane (Simpson) Robinson

This part of the family tree has its roots in Westmorland in the English Lake District, in particular in villages that straddle the valley of the River Eden between Penrith and Appleby, the latter town renowned since 1685 for its annual Romany horse fair.

John Robinson was the son of John and Mary (Hodgson) Robinson, both of whom had been born in Cliburn, Westmorland in 1764 and 1768 respectively, and who were married there in May 1789. After their marriage, they moved to Kirby Thore, where John was born in November 1801.

Jane was the second oldest of fifteen children from the marriage of John and Elizabeth (Williamson) Simpson, born in 1784 and 1785 respectively. They were married in Kirby Thore in November 1804, and moved into their farmstead home, The Red House, in Long Marton after their marriage. That property still stands in the main street of the village, its outbuildings to the rear now housing a microbrewery. Jane was born in The Red House in April 1807. She married John Robinson in Long Marton in June 1826, and lived in the village for another ten years before emigrating.

Seven of the Simpsons' children emigrated to Upper Canada. John S. Simpson was the first to go, arriving in Mosa Township in 1832. During the next decade, his brothers George, Edward, William and Isaac, together with John and Jane Robinson, and another sister Margaret and her husband Matthew Mitchell, all left their native Westmorland to build new lives for themselves in Mosa.

When they set off for Upper Canada, Jane was twenty-nine and John in his mid-thirties. They travelled with their three children; Anne, William and Mary. They set sail for New York from Liverpool on 17 May 1836. As was customary, their ship was most probably a vessel built to transport timber from North America to England, crudely converted to carry a human cargo on its return voyage. Family members' letters to their parents, John and Elizabeth (Williamson) Simpson, who remained in Long Marton, provide telling insights into their journeys and the various hardships they endured.

There is nothing on record to show that the Robinsons were beneficiaries of one of the assisted emigration schemes introduced around that time. Even if such assistance had been given, their journey to North America was made under less well planned and supervised conditions than their counterparts from Petworth and its surrounding villages in Sussex, whose formally assisted emigration, under the sponsorship of the Earl of Egremont, was a much more orderly and better financed affair. Possibly with limited financial help from the Simpson family, it is more likely that the Robinsons paid for their crossing. Their first letters home, written in November 1837, give a graphic description of their passage and circumstances on arrival.

They describe a voyage lasting six weeks, during which they weathered five severe storms and several members of their party (which included Jane's younger brother, Edward Simpson) suffered sickness. On arrival in New York on 26 June 1836, rations were low: 'We had very little spared excepting oatmeal and bacon', and they had very little money. On the night of their disembarkation, they took a steamboat heading north along the Hudson River, bound for Albany. They parted company with Edward there. They lacked the funds to continue their journey to Upper Canada: '... we could not go much farther for our money was near done.' The little money they had left was spent on fares for onward travel from Albany along the Mohawk River valley to Schenectady, before travelling on to Rotterdam, a few miles to the west, where they were to spend the next four and a half years.

Once in Rotterdam, John Robinson looked for work. Within a day of arrival, he was taken on as a labourer on the country estate of Mr Henry C. Yates who, in addition to his agricultural interests, had a law practice in New York. The terms of employment included a house for rent, firewood, monthly pay of $13, and ground in which they cultivated potatoes, other vegetables and apples, and on which they kept a fat hog. Their first letter, dated 15 November 1837, also included the following account of the local community:

People is very proud and dressey here the People are near all of them Duch We have not seen any Person from Westmorland yet Their is tow english men on the Farme from Yorkshire one of them was married when they came to this country the other has married a Duch Girl they have been near seven years hear there is a good many Black People hear We have never seen any Injins yet we suppose the solders are up West Driving them back.

The Robinsons were still in Rotterdam and not a little homesick when their next letter home was sent on 20 November 1838. It opens on a doleful note: 'You wished to know how I like a meric. I must tel you not as well as I expected for theire is hard times heare as well as England.' They had two more children, John and Margaret Elizabeth. It was also mentioned that William and Mary were attending school, for fees of 'a Doler each per quarter', and that Anne was old enough to have memories of Long Marton. Some of the children had contracted scarlet fever, but fortunately no-one had been affected by a local outbreak of smallpox which had resulted in many deaths.

John and Jane Robinson obviously had difficulty in accumulating the funds to enable them to travel on to Mosa, where other family members had settled. When they wrote home in January 1841, they were still in Rotterdam. However, they had moved into new accommodation close to their first home after John had left his job on the Yates' estate to work 'on the knell' (canal) for six shillings a day. Both homes they occupied in Rotterdam overlooked the Erie Canal, which provided a link between the Hudson River at Albany and Buffalo on Lake Erie. Since it was the main route to Upper Canada for emigrants arriving in New York, it must have been exceedingly frustrating for the Robinsons to witness that passing traffic.

Anne, William and, later, Mary had continued to attend school. By 1841, Anne had reached an age at which she had been sent out to work for $3 a month during the previous summer. The family's hardships had persisted and Jane's parents were thanked for money sent for their support. John and Jane had also suffered from 'the feavour and Ague' for two or three months, ill health they attributed to the poor quality of the water supply at their new home. Nevertheless, there was a glimmer of hope: 'If all be well in the Spring we think of moving to Youpper Canidy' (Upper Canada).

When William Simpson wrote home in December 1841, he mentioned that John Robinson was looking for a small farm in Mosa. In October 1842, his brother John Simpson reported the outcome of that search:

> John Robinson and his Family is living on a farm ajoining mine they find half the seed that they sow they have rented it for three Years they have to give one half of the Crops that they raise upon it for the rent they have all the farming utensils found them it does not take many in this Country John Robinson and a Neighbour have bought fourteen Acres of Wheat it is good I think they will have a good Bargain by it.

The Robinson family's struggle to establish themselves as independent farmers continued. Their daughter Anne's first letter to her grandparents, dated 20 January 1844, informed them that John and Jane had suffered further bouts of fever and ague during the first summer in Mosa, and she too 'had it for ten weeks and shook every day.' By then, her father was working John Simpson's farm on a half-share arrangement and had started to build up his stock, having acquired eight head of cattle, five hogs, seven geese and twenty hens. Apparently, from the same letter, Anne was unimpressed by Mosa: '... it is thinely seteled heare to what it was in the states I do not like this country so wel as the states we are to miles from any school I never saw a church since we moved up heare a Methodist minister preaches at one of our neighbours houses wonce in too weakes which we go to.'

After thanking her grandparents for gifts of clothing, needed because money was so scarce that settlers had to make their own cloth, Anne continued with her description of the township: '. . . thare are a great many wolves heare and some bears some of your neighbours wished to now what kind of houses we live in america in the states the huses are in general very good not so good heare as a great many of them are log buildings thare are some good brick houses and some frame buildings.'

There is no further trace of the Robinsons before the 1851 census of Canada West (as Upper Canada had been redesignated under the Act of Union, 1841). That census records John and Jane, living as farmer and wife with their children William, Mary, Margaret, and Elijah, born in 1843, after their arrival in Mosa, but not John, who is presumed to have died. Anne had married William Clements (junior), a son from my great great grandfather William Clements' first marriage, in or around 1847. They were living on the same or an adjacent lot with their two children, Mary Jane and John.

Anne (Robinson) Clements' second letter to her grandparents was written in 1857, a few years after the opening of the Great Western Railway route through Mosa Township, and the associated stimulus it provided for the development of the village of Newbury around its mainline station. Her letter reported that her parents were well, but gave no other news about them. Her brothers William and Elijah were still living in the family home. Her sister Mary had married Alex Armstrong, another of my great great grandfathers, in 1853. Anne was keener to pass on news of her own family, then numbering six, Mary Jane and John having been joined by William Robinson, George Byron, and twins Albert and Alfred. Her family's circumstances were described as follows:

> . . . we live in the village of Newbery we own a house and lot on the main street a short distence from the railroad a toun lot is a quarter of an acer land is a great deal dearer than it was before the railroad commenced town lots sel from too hundred to one thousand dolars each we let one large room this winter for 17 dolars my husband is working at framing and finishing a house.

William and Anne (Robinson) Clements moved on before the 1861 census was taken. However, John and Jane Robinson, then in their mid- to late-fifties, were still in Mosa in 1861. Isaac Simpson's letter home the following year confirmed that John Robinson had received a cheque for £27 from England, and reported that he had completed the construction of a brick built house that summer, a year in which the wheat harvest had been threatened by an infestation of weevils.

The last reference to the Robinsons in the Simpson Letters was in correspondence from William Simpson's daughter, Agnes, in June 1865, in which it was reported that John and his family remained in good health. Sadly, though, while John continued to farm for another five or six years, the registration of his death in February 1876, at the age of seventy-four years, noted it was preceded by five years of paralysis. Whether it was the result of accidental injury or a neurological disorder is not known.

From the will he signed in January 1875, it is apparent that John Robinson was intent to make provision for both Jane, who was made executrix, and their children. Jane, who passed away in 1878, was bequeathed the family home and contents, together with two lots comprising 100 acres, under the stipulation that, on her demise, she would in turn bequeath all to their youngest son, Elijah (which she did). His daughter Mary (Robinson) Armstrong was left a third lot of 50 acres. Her sisters Anne (Robinson) Clements and Margaret, who had married Alex Armstrong's older brother Charles, were each to inherit $200, to be paid on the second and fourth anniversaries, respectively, of their father's death. Other bequests were made to two grandsons, who would each receive $100 on reaching their eighteenth birthdays, and the estate of his son, William, who had predeceased him, which was to receive a half-acre plot from one of his holdings.

In many respects, the Robinsons' experience of emigration and adaptation to the 'new world' of Upper Canada, characterised as it was by privation, illness, frustration, constant struggle and dogged determination, is an archetypal pioneers' story. More affluent contemporaries, even those with just enough to reach their intended destination and pay a deposit on a lot, are likely to have endured less hardship. Nevertheless, the Robinsons can be said ultimately to have triumphed over adversity, and to have ended their days in more favourable circumstances than those in which they could have found themselves had they stayed in their native Westmorland.

Their survival was undoubtedly attributable to not just their own efforts but also the ongoing emotional and financial support from members of the extended family, both in Canada and more distantly in Westmorland. David Craig's *On the Crofters' Trail* describes the links forged between Scottish families who were compelled to emigrate by the Highland clearances and the relatives they left behind in Scotland – similar stories of family support, bridging the Atlantic and maintained via the rudimentary postal services of the day.

7

A Fermanagh Farmer

Like John Robinson, two other ancestors – my great great great grandfather Alexander Armstrong from Ireland and my great great grandfather William Clements from England – also set off for Upper Canada in the 1830s. Also like him, they were men of mature years with young families, who appear to have spent a few years elsewhere in North America before eventually settling in Mosa Township. One aspect of the Robinsons' legacy of a written record of emigration and settlement is the light it may incidentally shed on the likely early experiences of those other families, with whom eventually they were linked by marriage.

Alexander and Mary (Crawford) Armstrong

According to the inscription on the gravestone erected to his memory in the Old Cemetery, Wardsville, Alexander Armstrong lived to the age of 108 years. The official registration of his death in 1879, however, reports that he had reached the age of ninety-six, having been born in or around 1783.

Apart from evidence that Alexander Armstrong was from Magheracross in the civil parish of Ballinamallard, County Fermanagh, nothing else about his background has been discovered. From what is known about the pattern of settlement in that part of Ireland, it is quite probable that he was a descendant of the Armstrong clan from Liddesdale in the Scottish Borders who were known as 'reivers', a feared riding and raiding family. After the accession of

James VI (and I) to the English throne in 1603, the Armstrong clan's violent, lawless ways were perceived as a serious threat to his ambition to achieve the peaceful unification of his kingdoms of Scotland and England. As a result, steps were taken to force the Armstrongs into exile in Ireland, where many put down new roots in Fermanagh.

In the late eighteenth century, the rural society into which Alexander Armstrong was born mostly comprised tenant farmers and their families. Typically, those families farmed around 20 to 30 acres, on which crops of grain, potatoes and flax were grown alongside other land used for animal husbandry. Alexander Armstrong is most likely to have come from such a background.

Flax, used in the manufacture of linen, was important to that rural economy, since it was also the basis of a cottage spinning and handloom weaving industry. The industry was considered to be of sufficient significance to the local economy that, in 1796, the government supplied spinning wheels to farmers who grew flax, with those cultivating 5 acres or more also receiving a weaving loom. However, following the introduction of mechanised processes in purpose-built mills after 1820, the cottage industry rapidly declined. The consequential economic hardship could well have been one of the driving forces behind Alexander Armstrong's decision to emigrate.

Mary Crawford and Alexander Armstrong were married in Fermanagh in 1822. Mary (b. 1801) from Enniskillen was eighteen years younger than her husband. Their first child, a daughter, Frances, was born in 1822. Her birth was followed by those of Charles and Alex(ander), my great great grandfather. Those three children made the transatlantic crossing with their parents in or around 1830–31.

According to the digitised *Canadian County Atlas*, the Armstrong family arrived in Mosa Township in 1837. In the intervening years, the family spent time in Bytown, Carleton County and St Thomas in Elgin County. Before the family reached Mosa, three more children were born; John, William and Catherine. There is no first-hand information about the Armstrong family's early years in Mosa.

However, George Simpson, who also spent time in St Thomas working to accumulate the funds needed to settle in Mosa, described the state of development of the township in a letter to his father posted on 15 February 1835. He wrote that during the previous year he had spent ten weeks with his brother John, who had acquired a lot 'about 1 mile from Mosa' (i.e. Wardsville), which had two stores and a post office. John's lot was described in the following terms:

> He lives right on the river bank nearly about 100 yards from the river having about 4 acres of flat on the river the farm is well watered & all very good land excepting about 15 acres which is rather light and sandy nature there is a great deal of moss, excellent oak trees on it some bas wood, iron wood, ellem, Hickory, black & white ash, Maple, some cherry wood & wall nut trees.

Elsewhere, it is reported that he and John had cleared about 2 acres of forest, burning all except the wood spared for rail timber (fencing). They had also cut timber for John's house, which had been erected in a little over one day with neighbours' help, apart from its roof and finishing. George had dug out the cellar, which was twelve feet square and five feet deep, and helped his brother to sow an acre of wheat on the cleared land.

In contrast with his niece Anne (Robinson) Clements' perception of the township, George Simpson considered Mosa to be 'a well settled place'. Anne's views, of course, were coloured by the time her family had spent in the United States. Also John Simpson's lot was in the south of the township, the first part to be settled, whereas the Robinsons moved onto land to the north, at a time when it was still being 'opened up' for development.

After the family's arrival in Mosa, three more Armstrong sons were born; Hugh, James and Robert. When the 1851 census was taken, Alexander and Mary and their seven sons were still living together in one household. The oldest daughter, Frances, had already left home, having married Joseph Graham. (Their second son, Alexander Graham MD, was later to become one of the township's medical practitioners.) The younger daughter, Catherine, had been banished from the family, having offended her father's staunch Orange Order beliefs by falling in love with a young Roman Catholic man. It is rumoured that her lover was from the McLear family, whose story is told in the next chapter.

Land records show that Alexander did not secure title to the land on which he settled until June 1847. Though probably rough estimates, the 1851 agricultural census described a holding of approximately 140 acres, of which 40 were under cultivation and the remainder woodland. Half the cultivated land was pasture and the other used for growing wheat and oats. Stock included two horses, three bulls or steers, five milch (dairy) cows, seven calves or heifers, twenty sheep and nineteen pigs.

At that time, if born in 1783, Alexander would have been in his late sixties. It seems likely that his time was then spent overseeing the agricultural jobs performed by his older sons and hunting game for the table. If they had time, there would also have been plenty of opportunities for the Armstrong sons to work off the farm as labourers, saving additional earnings with a view to purchasing their own land at some future date. Alex, my great great grandfather, for example, worked on the construction of one of the area's log roads. Also, the arrival of the railroad in Newbury and the impetus it gave to the township's development, including the opening of a large timber mill, almost certainly provided an additional spur to woodland clearance and associated employment opportunities.

During the next decade, the four oldest sons married, with their roles on the family farm taken over by their three younger brothers who were still living in the family home in 1861. James, a life-long bachelor, and Robert were still with their parents in 1871, although Robert had married. Mary Armstrong died in March 1877, aged seventy-six years. Alexander Armstrong lived on for another two years, losing his life in a most horrific incident in April 1879. The official record of his death noted: 'The house in which deceased lived was burned and deceased was burned to death in it.' He had been smoking in bed.

Alexander Armstrong died intestate. His estate comprised 47 acres of land and the house in which he had lost his life, in which Robert and his family were still living. Within a few days, a quitclaim deed was drawn up. It is an interesting document, which was signed by all of Alexander's children (except Catherine, whose banishment was life-long) and their spouses. In it, they formally waived all claims they had on their father's estate and, in return for a nominal payment of $10, conveyed the property to Robert and his heirs and assignees in perpetuity.

That generosity toward their youngest brother was not out of place. He and his wife Mary had already been mainly responsible for the care their parents received in their old age, and Robert had also farmed the land on his father's behalf for many years. In any case, all of Robert's siblings were already comfortably established in their own properties and associated businesses. Most had become pillars of the township's community and had been active in its social, civic and religious affairs, the latter including the family's affiliations to the Anglican Church and the Orange Order, none more so than my great great grandfather, Alex Armstrong.

Alex and Mary (Robinson) Armstrong

Alex Armstrong and his wife Mary, the daughter of John and Jane (Simpson) Robinson, were married in Mosa in 1853. They had much in common. Both were born before their parents' emigration, Alex in County Fermanagh in 1829 and Mary in Westmorland in 1833, and had reached Mosa after periods of residence in other places, Alex in Upper Canada and Mary in the United States.

In 1851, both were still living with their parents, the census describing Alex as a twenty-one year old labourer and Mary as a seventeen year old daughter. Their first child, my great grandmother, Mary Ann, was born in September 1854. The 1861 census recorded

Alex and Mary as living on a shared lot in Mosa with his younger brother William and his wife Isabella. Another daughter, Jane, had been born in 1857.

During the next decade, five more children were born – Joseph, Frances, Hugh, Matthew and Margaret. It was a period during which Alex began to amass quite extensive land holdings and in which he first served as Deputy to the Reeve, the township's most senior, elected, municipal officer.

In 1871, all seven children were living with their parents – six were still there ten years later. The exception was Mary Ann, who had married my great grandfather, Thomas Clements, in 1876. Two years later, the mapping of land holdings in Mosa Township showed that in total Alex Armstrong held in the region of 500 acres. He had also continued in office as Deputy Reeve.

The 1880s though, brought many changes. Jane, Joseph and Frances married and left home. And in March 1889 Mary passed away, aged fifty-five years. A year later, Alex Armstrong married for the second time. His bride, Mary Ann Burgess, was a forty-four year old widow with two sons, Joseph and John. She had accompanied her English parents to Canada in 1848. She is remembered as a strong adherent to the Plymouth Brethren sect who converted Alex and some of his descendents to her evangelical faith. Thus, in the 1891 census, in contrast with earlier reports of his English Church (Anglican) affiliation, Alex's religion was recorded as 'Believer in Christ'. That year, in addition to Mary Ann and her two sons, Hugh, Matthew and Margaret were still at home with their father, although the latter two were soon to depart when they too married. By 1901, Alex's stepsons had also left home, leaving only Hugh with his father and stepmother. Alex was still associated with the Plymouth Brethren sect, and presumably remained so until his death in April 1904, aged seventy-five years.

Alex Armstrong shines through the records as a patriarchal figure, an industrious man who amassed considerable wealth and participated actively in the township's civic affairs. His sons and all but one of his daughters (Margaret, whose husband William Stokes was a railroad agent) followed the family tradition of farming, almost certainly assisted by a father who either passed on some of his own land or contributed to the purchase of their holdings. The Plymouth Brethren sect also benefited from his largesse; he financed the construction of its meeting house in Newbury. However, his family's adherence to that faith is said to have been responsible for long-standing ill feelings and a lack of communication between the Armstrong family and those in other branches of the family tree.

8

A Wiltshire Day Labourer

For quite a long time, the earliest trace of my great great grandfather, William Clements, was provided by the 1851 census of Canada West. That source located him and his family in Mosa Township and indicated that he had been born in England around 1800, but offered no clues about his birthplace or the circumstances leading to, or date of, his emigration.

The key that eventually unlocked William Clements' past was the serendipitous discovery that a letter sent to his father a few months after his arrival in Upper Canada had survived. The letter had originally been included in an 1831 pamphlet, *Extracts of Letters from Poor Persons who Emigrated Last Year to Canada and the United States*, containing similar correspondence. It was edited by George Poulett Scrope, Member of Parliament for Stroud and a fervent advocate of assisted emigration schemes, and brought to my attention through a reference in a more recent article on assisted emigration by Dr Gary Howells, published in the journal *History* in 2003.

The pamphlet identified William Clements' birthplace as the Wiltshire parish of Corsley. In 1800, Corsley had a population of 1,412, which increased to 1,729 by 1831, the increase being partly attributable to an influx of workers employed in the village's textile mills. At the same time, following the enclosure of common land by the Marquis of Bath in 1783, the parish had an increasing number of paupers for whose needs it had to cater. Records indicate that during the 1820s, and in particular between 1829 and 1831, around 200 Corsley inhabitants emigrated to North America. Included in that number was a party of sixty-six 'undesirables' whose emigration in

1830 was aided by parish funds and assistance from the Marquis of Bath, whose ancestral estate, Longleat, marked Corsley's southern boundary.

William and Mary (Cook) Clements

Canadian and American records suggest that William Clements was born in or around 1800, but it is possible he was born a little earlier. His parents were John and Mary Clements. John Clements was still alive when the 1841 census was taken, but missing from the 1851 count. Mary's fate is unknown. The parish Overseer's Account Book listed John Clements amongst the 'constant poor' throughout the 1820s and beyond, indicating that his later years were spent as a pauper dependent on parish relief.

William Clements married his first wife, Mary Cook (b. 1801), in Corsley's parish church in September 1822. Their first child was a son, John. He was born in 1823, but did not survive infancy. John was followed by William and George, who both emigrated to Upper Canada with their parents. Their names and dates of birth were instrumental in confirming that the 'William Clements' mentioned in English, Canadian and, later, United States' records were one and the same person.

George Poulett Scrope described William Clements as an agricultural day labourer. With no common land available after enclosure, there would have been little or no scope for even the modest self-sufficiency his Georgian peasant farming forebears are likely to have achieved. Consequently, he would have depended for a living on casual or seasonal farm work when available.

A description of the Wiltshire countryside of this time and the precarious state of the county's labouring population can be found in William Cobbett's *Rural Rides*. On Friday 1 September 1826, he started his day by providing breakfast for a party of eight unemployed cloth workers from Bradford on Avon who had been gathering nuts for their sustenance. Having spent the morning travelling from Heytesbury to Warminster, Cobbett journeyed on to Frome along a route that took him across the southern reaches of the parish of Corsley. He recorded his reaction to the extreme poverty he had witnessed during that day's travel:

> I am really ashamed to ride a fat horse, to have a full belly, and to have a clean shirt on my back, while I look at these wretched countrymen of mine; while I actually see them reeling with weakness; when I see their poor faces present me with nothing but skin and bone, while they are toiling to get the wheat and the meat ready to be carried away by the tax-eaters (Cobbett's term for the absentee lay and clergy landlords).

He was similarly stirred by the sight of paupers who had been set to work to 'earn' their entitlement to parish relief that greeted him on reaching Frome: '… where I saw upon my entrance to the town, between two and three hundred weavers, men and boys, cracking stones, moving earth, and doing other types of work, towards making a fine road into the town.'

On the subject of assisted emigration, a contentious political issue at that time, William Cobbett and George Poulett Scrope were poles apart. In contrast with the latter's fervent support for such schemes, Cobbett railed against the 'schemers' on the Emigration Committee and sided with those who advocated deployment on local public works as the preferred alternative.

Corsley, with its similar dependence on agricultural labour and the cloth trade, would have been just as prone to that toxic mix of high unemployment or underemployment and grinding poverty which, four years after Cobbett's rides through Wiltshire, triggered widespread rural revolt in the form of the Swing Riots. There can be little doubt the landowners and other members of the establishment sensed the increasing frustration and desperation of the rural poor, and were careful to identify potential troublemakers and their ringleaders. It would not be at all surprising to learn that William Clements was seen to belong to the latter category, and that it was that perceived threat and not a long record of dependence on the parish for relief which led to his inclusion in the party of Corsley's residents, the 'undesirables', who, through sums raised by the sale of property in the parish and a £50 donation from the Marquis of Bath, were assisted to emigrate to Upper Canada in 1830.

When times were hard, William Clements could have been obliged to seek help from Corsley's Poor Law Overseer. Indeed, it is clear from the latter's accounts, in which William's name was listed among the 'occasional poor' during the last four months of the 1829–30 accounting year, when he received in total £2.16s.10d, that he was briefly dependent on such relief. But that sum was far less than the amounts awarded to many others including, for example, Esau Prangley, listed among the occasional poor both at that time and throughout the whole of the preceding year, and who emigrated to Upper Canada at the same time.

Whatever the reasons for their departure, that party of sixty-six adults and children set off in wagons to Bristol where, it has been reported, some were reluctant to board ship and required a measure of force to detain them. Apparently, as a further precaution, the vessel was sailed across the Bristol Channel to Newport in Monmouthshire before its eventual departure in the spring of 1830. On arrival, the party dispersed. From Poulett Scrope's pamphlet, it is known that some made their way to Dummer Township in Peterborough County, where they would have become comparatively close neighbours to *Roughing it in the Bush* author Susannah Moodie and her family. For William Clements and a few others, the intended destination was Southwold Township on the northwestern shore of Lake Erie, where Daniel Silcox, a former Corsley resident, had secured a 200-acre lot in 1824.

Within months of their arrival, Esau Prangley and William Clements wrote letters home. Both were postmarked Port Talbot, Upper Canada and dated 30 October 1830, a coincidence that could indicate they made use of the services of a scribe associated with the post office. In his letter, Esau Prangley reported:

We arrived last July, and like the country well. Clements and I have bought 100 acres of land between us. We have about 25 acres cleared on my 50, for £70. I have paid down £12.10s. and I have 5 years to pay the remainder in. I have a house and a barn on the place ready to go into. I have sowed 4½ acres of wheat.

Scrope's extracts from William Clements' letter were as follows:

My dear Father, I thank God I am got to the land of liberty and plenty. I arrived here on the 9th July. I had not a single shilling left when I got here. But I met with good friends that took me in; and I went to work at 6s. per day and my board on to this day. And now I am going to work on my Farm of 50 acres, which I bought at £55, and have 5 years to pay it. I have bought me a Cow and 5 pigs. And I have sowed 4½ acres of Wheat, and I have 2 more to sow. I am going to build me a house this fall, if I live. And if I had staid at Corsley, I never should have had nothing. I like the country very much. I am at liberty to shoot turkeys, quail, pigeon, and all kinds of game which I have in my back wood. I have also a sugar bush, that will make me a ton of sugar yearly. The timber is very fine. We sow but one bushel of wheat to an acre, and the increase is about 50. One single grain will bring from 30 to 60 ears. The land in general is black peat and sandy loam. My wife and two sons is all well and happy, and thankful that they are arrived over safe; and wish father and mother and all the family were as well provided for as we be. If the labouring men did but know the value of their strength, they would never abide contented in the old country. Cows are worth from 50s. to £3.10s. Sheep, large and fat is worth 10s.6d . Oxen from £5 to £6. No poor-rate, no taxes, no overseer, no beggars. The wheat that is left in the fields would keep a whole parish. Several of them that came out with us are near, Joseph Silcox within 2 miles, &c.

It's not known precisely where William Clements and his family first settled, but there are indications that they were in the vicinity of Iona village, Dunwich Township, close to the boundary with Southwold. In another of Scrope's compilation of emigrants' letters, William Singer, a bricklayer from Corsley, writing home from Southwold in March 1831, reported: 'We have eight families within 2 miles all from Westbury and Corsley.'

William and Mary (Cook) Clements moved on, although when and why are not known. Their names were not found in the 1842 censuses of Dunwich and Southwold. After their arrival in Upper Canada, William and Mary had six more children; Mary, Ann, Elizabeth, Jane, Rachel and John. For a time, it seemed that John was the first child from a second marriage; in the 1900 United States Federal Census he reported his mother's country of origin as Ireland. But that turned out to be his father's second wife, the woman with whom he spent his childhood, not the one who had given birth to him. The records of the Cameron Church in Mosa, where Mary (Cook) Clements was interred, have been lost, but it would seem that his mother died either in childbirth when John was born in 1846, or quite soon after.

In April 1848, on payment of full fees and associated administrative costs, William Clements was formally assigned a lot in Mosa. The Free Grant gave him the right to occupy the lot, but did not confer ownership. Like Alexander Armstrong, he might have settled there unofficially as much as a decade earlier, as part of the group who are known to have migrated from Dunwich to Mosa in the late 1830s. From the 1851 agricultural census, he was certainly quite well established by that date. The family lived in a log house. Around one half of the lot's 97 acres was under cultivation with 34 acres of crops, including wheat, oats and potatoes, and 15 acres of pasture. The remaining acreage was woodland. The family had yet to acquire a horse, but other stock included two bulls or steers, four dairy cows and six calves or heifers, four sheep, and eight pigs.

The population census for the same year reflected William Clements' second marriage to Margaret McLear in 1847. Family members listed included all but one of the eight children from the first marriage. The oldest son, William, had married Anne Robinson and was living elsewhere in the township. There were also three children from the second marriage – Thomas, my great grandfather, Henry and Margaret.

During the 1850s, apart from the youngest, John, the children from William Clements' first marriage left Mosa Township. Spearheaded by George, the second oldest son, all moved to the United States, where they resettled, married and brought up families of their own in the state of Michigan.

William and Margaret (McLear) Clements

Margaret McLear was born in County Tyrone in 1816. Her parents were Hugh and Roseanna (O'Conor) McLear. In addition to Margaret, they had at least four other children. Though there is no record of their transatlantic crossing, they travelled to Canada as a family in the late 1840s.

The family, who were staunch Roman Catholics, first settled in Ekfrid Township before moving to Euphemia, where their presence was recorded by the 1861 and 1871 censuses. Hugh McLear was a weaver. He passed away in 1876, four years after his wife's death. They were laid to rest in Wardsville Old Martyrs' Cemetery, as were most of their children.

After 1851, four more children were added to William and Margaret (McLear) Clements' family. They were Patrick, Richard, Maria and Mary. The 1861 census recorded all except Mary with their parents, together with John, the youngest member of William's first family. Sadly, that arrangement was not long lasting. At some point after Mary's birth in 1863, the marriage failed because Margaret adamantly refused to convert from her Roman Catholic faith to William's Anglican beliefs.

It must have been a most serious difference of opinion. William's response was to desert his young second family. Possibly accompanied by John, who also left Mosa around that time, he followed his older children to Michigan, never to return or have any other dealings with the young family he left behind. The United States Federal Censuses in 1870 and 1880 revealed that he was living at his son George's home in Van Buren County. Evidently, his listing in the 1871 Canadian census was a fabrication, no doubt motivated by Margaret's need to hang on to the family's lot in Mosa, for which they had yet to secure full ownership. The absentee William's listing as a 'Roman Catholic' in that census was perhaps either a belated gesture to save his soul or an act of exquisite revenge on the deserted wife's part.

Because census data for Michigan in 1890 is fragmentary, William Clements' precise whereabouts at that time are not known. Nevertheless, it is apparent from his neglected, lichen-encrusted gravestone in the cemetery at Carson City, Michigan that his final years were spent with his daughter Jane and her husband, John McQuaig, just over the county line in North Shade, Gratiot County. He died there in 1894.

Meanwhile, Margaret was left with her children to raise. The digitised 1878 map of land holdings in Mosa showed my great grandfather Thomas and his brother Henry as occupiers of two adjacent lots, totalling 97 acres. In 1881, Margaret and her children Henry, Richard, Maria and Mary were still on one of those lots. Her daughter, Margaret (a.k.a. Maggie) had died in 1875, and Patrick had left home, having also obtained his own lot to farm before 1878. He later went on to farm in Enniskillen Township, Lambton County.

Henry, who was still farming alongside his mother in 1891, later went to British Columbia with his younger brother Richard. Both were bachelors and are said to have found work on the railroad. A photograph taken around the time they headed west has survived. Maria is remembered as a spinster, whose son, Frederick, was born out of wedlock. He was living with his grandmother in 1891 and 1901. Maria was a seamstress who spent part of her working life in Michigan. Although there was no further news of Richard, his sister Maria and Henry are known to have been alive in 1939. In a letter to the family in Mosa, they wrote that they were sharing a home and thinking about returning to the township. The fate of their youngest sister, Mary, has proved elusive. She may have passed away in her twenties. Thus, by 1901, Margaret (McLear) Clements was left to share her home with one grandson. She passed away there in 1905, in her eighty-ninth year.

Thomas and Mary Ann (Armstrong) Clements

These are my other paternal great grandparents. They were born in Mosa, Thomas in August 1848 and Mary Ann in September 1854. Their parents were near neighbours. Before their marriage in 1876, Thomas Clements worked as a farm labourer for Mary Ann's father, Alex Armstrong. A quitclaim deed records that, on 14 April 1873, Thomas purchased for $700 the lot on which his father had settled and had been granted the right to occupy without benefit of ownership.

The purchase of the lot, and the construction on it of a house which Thomas and Mary Ann occupied after their marriage, would probably not have been possible without financial assistance from the bride's father. Their first child, Margaret, was born there in 1878. She was followed by Hugh, Frances, Edith, Charles (my grand-father), Alexander and Thomas. There was also another daughter, Millie, who died in infancy.

In 1881, Thomas and Mary Ann and their first two children were occupying one-half of the Clements' lot, as neighbours to his mother and younger siblings. Ten years later, their family had increased to five children, and only Henry was still with his mother on the next door half lot. By 1901, the two youngest children had been born, and they were all together as a family unit. Thomas' mother, who was to pass away four years later, was still on the adjoining property with only a grandson for company. Around that time, after Henry's departure to British Columbia, and with his mother in her eighties, Thomas appears to have re-combined the two halves of the original lot.

Only the three youngest sons were living at home in 1911. Their brother Hugh had left to marry and work on his own farm. The three daughters had also left home to marry, Frances and Edith doing so under more conventional circumstances than their older sister Margaret. In 1903, Margaret gave birth to a son, Clarence, out of wedlock. The story passed down over the years is that the father was a local man of First Nation descent who refused to 'do the right thing' by agreeing to marry. Apparently, Margaret's mother, Mary Ann, was so incensed by his behaviour she put a curse on him, a curse that was believed to have found expression after his marriage to another woman, who gave birth to a child who was both deaf and dumb. Margaret did find another partner, Benjamin Miller, and Thomas and Mary Ann raised Clarence as their son. Margaret died in Mosa in 1913, around the time of her son's tenth birthday. Like Hugh, my grandfather's other brothers, Alexander and Thomas, spent their working lives as farmers, and Frances and Edith also married men from farming families.

Mary Ann died in Mosa in October 1917, aged sixty-four years. Her death registration noted the cause as a twenty-year history of diabetes. Thomas survived for another twenty-two years. He retired from farming in the early 1920s, passing on or selling the family's lot to his son Alexander. In the registration of the death of a prematurely-born infant in September 1923, that lot was recorded as Alexander's address, suggesting that the transfer of ownership could have been completed before that date.

Throughout his later years, Thomas Clements was in the habit of over-wintering with Alexander and his family. He is also understood to have used those years to share some of his remaining wealth with other sons, including my grandfather, Charles. Thomas met an untimely and tragic end in July 1939 when, just two weeks short of his ninety-first birthday (and not his ninety-third as reported), he was the victim of a railroad accident less than a quarter of a mile from his home. On 27 July 1939, the front page of *The Glencoe Transcript* carried the following report of that tragic event:

Thomas Clements, aged 93, of Newbury was instantly killed on Wednesday morning last week when the horse and buggy which he was driving was struck by a fast CPR passenger train. Mr Clements was driving north in an open horse-drawn buggy at the first crossing east of North Newbury station and failed to notice the approach of the east-bound flyer. The horse was just across the tracks and the buggy directly in the path of the train when struck. The buggy was completely demolished and Mr Clements tossed in the air and was picked up 200 feet east of the crossing. He was dead when reached. Andrew Armstrong, a nephew of Mr Clements, was working in a nearby field and attempted to signal his uncle and warn him of the approaching train, but was unable to get the attention of the man. Coroner Dr Lockwood, of Newbury, was called to the scene immediately after the crash, which occurred at 10.23 a.m. Mr Clements is survived by four sons and two daughters; Thomas, Alex, Hugh and Charles Clements of Brooke township, Mrs John Graham of Alvinston, and Mrs John Mitchell of Petrolia.

Charles and Ethel Rebecca (Babcock) Clements

The final intertwining of the diverse strands of paternal ancestry was marked by my grandparents' marriage, the official record of which had been the starting point for these enquiries into my father's forebears. Ethel Babcock's roots were predominantly Anglo-Scottish-Irish, but with an additional, distant 'seasoning' of Dutch and German on her father's side. Charles Clements, on the other hand, descended from mainly Anglo-Irish stock.

Ethel, daughter of Joseph and Elizabeth (Watson) Babcock, was born in Ompah, Palmerston North Township in December 1892, the fourth of her parents' six children. In the early 1900s, her family, accompanied by her grandfather Alexander Watson, moved to Mosa Township. When the 1911 census was taken, she was eighteen years old and still living her with parents. Her future husband Charles, the son of Thomas and Mary Ann (Armstrong) Clements, a twenty-five year old bachelor and labourer, was living nearby on the lot that his father had farmed since the 1870s.

My grandparents 'tied the knot' in November 1913 in Walkerville, now part of Windsor. The record reports that Charles, still a labourer, had been living in Walkerville for the previous six months. Ethel's address (after a crossing out of Walkerville) was given as Newbury.

The reasons for the choice of Walkerville were not particularly obvious. It was tempting to speculate that the proposed marriage might not have received parental approval, prompting an elopement. Alternatively, it might simply have reflected economic imperatives: the likelihood that, as a younger son, Charles would not 'inherit' the family's lot, and the attraction of better-paid employment in the industries that were then being established in and around Windsor, such as the newly-opened Ford Motor Company plant.

They did not stay in Walkerville. When their first child, Charles Fay, was born in 1916, they were living near Shetland in Lambton County. In addition to Charles Fay and my father, Max, there were four other children – Coralie, Marilyn, Shirley Ann, and Thomas – some of whom lived in Lambton County and others more distantly in New Jersey and British Columbia. But that was just about all I had learned about my paternal grandparents before I decided to travel to Canada in 2007. What more was there to be discovered?

9

My Father's Family

After my first visit to Canada in 2007, I acquired a much more detailed picture of my paternal grandparents and the life they lived. My grandmother, Ethel Rebecca Babcock, completed her elementary education in Mosa in 1905, and remembered Margaret (McLear) Clements' death during that year. She met my grandfather, Charles Clements, in or around 1906 at house parties, social occasions with music and dancing at which young people from the widely-scattered farms could meet and socialise. In her mid-teenage years, she used to go to parties with her older sister, Emma, who was then courting Ernest Armstrong (one of Alex Armstrong's grandsons). My grandfather fell for Ethel, and was charged with responsibility for escorting her home while older house party guests enjoyed their evening entertainments.

However, the occasion of Emma and Ernest Armstrong's marriage in 1907 became a source of bad blood between their families. Apparently, some Armstrong family members, who expected to be invited in large numbers, vehemently objected to the suggested presence on the proposed guest list of some of the bride's family members, including one of her mother's brothers. So it would appear that my grandparents' decision to marry in Walkerville was not an elopement but, rather, motivated by a desire to avoid a repetition of inter-family strife.

For a short time after they married in November 1913, my grandparents lived with John and Edith (Clements) Mitchell, who had acted as their witnesses at the wedding. But they soon found a property of their own near the Ford plant, the first of Henry Ford's factories to be built outside the United States, where my grandfather had already found employment. They lived off money my grandmother earned from taking in boarders, some of which was used to furnish their home, while saving my grandfather's income to achieve their goal of farm ownership. Some of the items of furniture they bought, which have passed down the family and still grace one of their great granddaughter's homes, attest to the care with which they have been treated for almost a century.

Their move into farming may have been brought forward by my grandfather's reported desire to avoid conscription after the outbreak of war in 1914. Quite soon afterwards, they returned to Mosa, where they briefly stayed with my grandfather's parents. Seemingly, my grandmother didn't find her mother-in-law especially kind or friendly. They were occupying their first, presumably rented, farm in Shetland in Lambton County by July 1916, when their first child, Charles Fay, was born. Coralie, the second child and mother of my cousin Beth, was also born in Shetland in 1918.

My grandparents farmed there until April 1919, when they bought a 100-acre lot adjoining that of my great grandparents, Joseph and Elizabeth (Watson) Babcock. The price was $5,350, to be repaid in annual instalments over ten years. When they came to sell the farm to Emerson Kelly in March 1925, they still owed $2,983.34. During my grandparents' ownership of that farm, two more children were born, Marilyn in 1922 and my father, Max, in 1924. My father's birthplace, at 2549 CPR Drive, Newbury (its modern postal address) was still standing in 2010, but unoccupied and under threat of demolition.

My grandfather found that the farm had poor quality sandy soil, so he looked for an alternative. In 1925, he bought another 100-acre property with good land in Brooke Township, for which he needed a $10,000 mortgage, agreed privately with a local man. While there, my grandparents' two youngest children were born – Shirley Ann and Thomas. However, their time in Brooke Township coincided with the Wall Street crash of 1929 and the early years of the Great Depression.

Just before those calamitous events, my grandfather received a gift of $1,000 from his father. But that gift appears to have created a family rift between my grandfather and at least one of his brothers, since he believed that brother played a part in events that were to end his ownership of the farm for which he and his wife had worked so hard. By 1932, they had managed to reduce their mortgage debt to around $4,000. But with the effects of deep economic recession blighting businesses everywhere, the following year brought severe financial hardship to all farmers, and their plight undoubtedly set alarm bells ringing among those who had loaned capital to them. So, though my grandfather managed to pay the interest on his mortgage in 1933, he was unable pay off any of the outstanding capital debt. A malicious rumour that he was about to renege on that debt began to circulate. My grandfather believed that his youngest brother had started the rumour and had been instrumental in bringing it to the lender's attention. He was so enraged and felt so betrayed, he never spoke to his brother again.

For my grandparents, the final straw came at Christmas 1933, when they had to cope with foreclosure of the private mortgage on their farm. The ruinous outcome, in which they forfeited their entire investment, was mitigated only by a moonlight flight across the Lambton-Middlesex county boundary in which the older children and Babcock relatives helped to save the family's livestock, farm equipment and other moveable possessions. At my first meeting with Joe Babcock, he described his own role in leading one of the horse and cart teams used that night.

The family's troubles did not end there. The first quarter of 1934 was spent in temporary accommodation on Shields Sidings Drive, Mosa, just a few hundred yards from the property of the lender responsible for the loss of their farm and livelihood. Sadly, just a few months later – too late for my grandparents – the Canadian government decided to provide some support for its struggling farmers. It had been a most distressing time for all, not least my grandfather, who was driven to attempt to take his own life, only to be thwarted by my grandmother's intervention. It was their darkest hour; its effect on my father and his siblings is not difficult to envisage.

In April 1934, my grandparents found a new farm to rent in Glen Rae, a hamlet in Enniskillen Township, Lambton County. But their troubles continued. That year, the harvest failed and my grandmother, with her very young family to care for, was forced to find work to raise the cash to buy seed for the next year's crops. They worked the Glen Rae property until the owner decided to sell it in November 1937.

Their search for yet another farm to rent resulted in a move to a larger property to the south of Watford. It was there, in 1941, they decided to end their involvement in farming. My grandfather was then aged fifty-five years and, given his earlier disappointments, probably didn't relish the prospect of a continuing struggle. After selling their livestock and farm implements, they moved to a house in Park Street, Strathroy with sufficient land for my grandfather to grow stock, mostly soft fruit, for a local nursery, where he was also employed as a nurseryman. He ended his working life in that job.

In 1953, after his retirement, my grandparents made their last move to a small clapboard house on Eureka Street in Petrolia, where his life-long love of plants found expression in the cultivation of seedlings and the tending of his small vegetable plot. A gentle man with a quiet disposition, and with a string of disappointments in his wake, he died in 1961, aged seventy-five years.

My grandmother, a petite, feisty, proud and fiercely independent woman, and undoubtedly the partner from whom the marriage acquired most of its strength, outlived her husband by a considerable margin. At her death in 1992, she was in her 100th year. She had retained her independence in shopping, housework and personal care well into her late nineties. There is no better indication of her pride and independence than my father's discovery on one of his visits that many of the packets and other food containers in her seemingly well-stocked cupboards were empty. Obviously, she hoped to convey a very different impression to less curious visitors.

With the benefit of hindsight, it is apparent that my grandparents' move into small-scale farming was made at the least propitious time. After the First World War, small farms became increasingly expensive to run. If farmers were to make a reasonable living, trends of increased mechanisation and decreased labour called for significant investment in machinery and larger land holdings. The pattern of farming in that area throughout the nineteenth and into the first two decades of the twentieth century was doomed to fragment, paving the way for the evolution of today's agribusiness corporations. The consequences for Charles and Ethel (Babcock) Clements, their children, and their cousins in other branches of the family tree (indeed, for Canadian farming communities more generally) were evident in steps their government took to foster the diversification of rural economies and the migration of farm labour to different occupations in towns and cities.

The lives of my father's brothers and sisters were certainly touched by those macroeconomic developments. His older brother, Charles Fay, spent his life in Petrolia, where he worked as a motor mechanic before starting his own vehicle servicing and repair business. The oldest sister, Coralie, who also lived nearby, married a man who developed other business interests alongside his farming. Marilyn trained as a beautician and spent her adult years in Toronto, where she also ran her own business. Shirley Ann, my father's only surviving sibling, completed high school and college before qualifying as a teacher. But after five years she looked for a career change and found it in an Air Canada job, which took her to New York. Thomas (a.k.a. Bud), my father's youngest sibling, died in 2010 after several years of debilitating illness. After failing to find a permanent niche in the adverse conditions of the post-Second World War labour market, he enlisted in the Canadian Army, in which he served for ten years. On discharge, he lived with his parents in Petrolia for a time, before leaving to spend the rest of his life in British Columbia, where he found employment in the forestry industry before suffering a disabling injury, which resulted in the loss of use of one arm. Thomas fell out of favour with his siblings following a dispute over his parents' property, and thereafter had little or no involvement with them.

My father

Max Hubert Clements was born on 3 December 1924 in the family farm next to his grandparents' lot on CPR Drive, Newbury. He had an inauspicious start to life. Believing he was stillborn, the midwife laid him to one side in order to look after his mother. It was only when he showed signs of life that attention was redirected to him. During the year after his birth, his family moved into the farm in Brooke Township, where they were to remain until around his ninth birthday. A school photograph taken about 1931–32, in which he and his fellow pupils were barefooted, is a telling portrayal of rural poverty. The experience of going without shoes made a lasting impression, and is said to explain my father's life-long obsession with good quality footwear for both his family and himself.

Undoubtedly, the enforced abandonment of the farm in Brooke Township, followed by several moves in quick succession had unsettling effects on the whole family. They were years during which my father progressed from boyhood to adolescence, but moving around had disrupted his education. His school after the move to Glen Rae was the third he had attended that year. That experience did not whet his appetite for formal education, from which he increasingly distanced himself.

Also, as he entered adolescence, his father expected him to contribute toward his keep by working on the farm for little or no tangible reward. My Aunt Shirley has recalled that those demands caused friction between father and son, to which, while still very young, my father reacted by leaving home to live and work on neighbouring farms where, presumably, he was better paid. In her view, my grandfather was the loser in that battle of wills and the loss of my father's help was a major factor in his decision to sell up and quit farming altogether in 1941. Aunt Shirley also attributes my father's decision to ignore his own father's needs and go his own way to an independent – if not stubbornly determined – streak that was a hallmark of his character.

Perhaps my father enlisted in the army for mixed motives – a youthful desire to serve his country and the prospect of increased independence. Certainly, at the time, he would not have been alone in perceiving enlistment as a means of escape from the hardship, drudgery and monotony of a depressed rural economy. Whatever his reasoning, he made his first attempt to enlist in early 1941, soon after his sixteenth birthday, but was thwarted by his parents' intervention. Appreciating the seriousness of his intent, they did not oppose his second attempt later that year, when enlistment formalities for Private A-62255 M. H. Clements were rubber-stamped in London, Ontario on 11 July 1941.

The new recruit was assigned to the Royal Canadian Army Service Corps, with a posting to Camp Debert, Nova Scotia for training. That training proceeded over the ensuing year as the 4th Canadian Armoured Division, to which his Petrol Company was attached, prepared for its eventual transfer to Europe. The photograph of my father, received in response to the enquiries addressed to my cousin Beth, dates from that time, as does cine film footage of him in uniform in Petrolia, one of a series of similar vignettes of local recruits, recording their enlistment for posterity. In Halifax, in September 1942, he boarded the troopship that sailed to Britain, where his company disembarked in Liverpool in early October, before onward transfer to Aldershot.

The 4th Canadian Armoured Division's training continued at Aldershot and Heathfield, Sussex until August 1943, when it was relocated to East Anglia, where it participated in other exercises to the year's end, before returning to Sussex. (It was during that relocation to East Anglia that my mother and father met.) Back in the southeast, my father's division took part in other training exercises in readiness for its role in Operation Overlord, the invasion of northern France, for which planning was then well advanced.

Unless the Canadian authorities remove or modify the legislative barriers that preclude me from accessing my father's army records, details of his personal involvement in the conflict that resulted in Germany's surrender in 1945 will not be revealed. The alternative is to rely on the more general narrative provided in historical records and accounts. Those sources indicate that the 4th Canadian Armoured Division did not take part in the D-Day landings. Rather, it was held in reserve until beachheads in Normandy had been secured and did not cross the English Channel until July 1944. Once in France, the division – part of the Canadian First Army – was deployed in breaking the enemy's stronghold in and around Caen and the onward thrust toward Falaise, which fell into allied hands in mid-August.

After that, Canadian forces comprised the most northerly of the allied thrusts into France, advancing along a route that shadowed the coastline first to the River Seine and then into Belgium. By October, they were embroiled in a five-week long battle to wrest the River Scheldt delta in northern Belgium from enemy control, thereby opening the port of Antwerp, already in British hands, for allied shipping and creating a more secure, less extended line of supply. In those engagements, in which Canadian forces suffered heavy casualties, my father's division was in action in clearing ground around the Dutch town of Breskens and establishing a bridgehead over the Ghent Canal at Moerbrugge. After a setback in a similar attempt to establish a bridgehead over the Leopold Canal near Moerkerke, the division moved north to take the town of Bergen-op-Zoom.

From there, in December 1944, the epicentre of conflict shifted eastward to the Ardennes, where Germany mounted a counter-attack, albeit unsuccessfully. After wintering south of the River Maas, the Canadian First Army's actions were focussed on the territory between the Maas and the Rhine east of Nijmegen, with an expectation that it would advance through Reichswald Forest on the Dutch-German border. The subsequent clearance of that border took the First Army north via Arnhem in early April 1945. The 4th Canadian Armoured Division's objectives were to seize the town of Almelo, before crossing the frontier near Neuenhaus and Emlichen in a finger of German territory that pointed westward into Holland. That mission was accomplished on 5 April, and paved the way for an onward move into the north German plain. The division crossed the River Ems near Meppen on 7 April before advancing on Old-enburg, via Sogel and Friesoythe, mopping up pockets of resistance on the way. The end of the war was in sight. On 29 April, German forces in Italy surrendered. Adolf Hitler committed suicide the next day. German forces in northwest Europe surrendered uncondi-tionally on 4 May. Victory in Europe (VE) Day was celebrated four days later.

When pressed by Marlene in his later years, my father mentioned that his unit had reached Oldenburg. While his precise whereabouts on VE Day are unclear, his experiences on that day are not. Having survived the war physically unscathed, his celebratory participation in a stunt involving several fellow soldiers, a cache of alcohol and a motorcycle resulted in a broken leg. In a company photograph, taken in June 1944 before embarkation to France, my father was wearing a lance corporal's stripe. The rank recorded in his discharge papers was that of private. Without access to the relevant records, the reason for that demotion remains a mystery. But was it by any chance attributable to his involvement in the motorcycle escapade? My father himself had confessed that he was airlifted from a field hospital in Germany to Colchester in Essex for treatment and convalescence. While there, his division withdrew to Holland to await transportation home.

My father returned to Canada aboard the *Mauretania*, which docked in Halifax on 9 December 1945. From there, he made his way to Strathroy, to the family home into which his parents had moved after selling off their farming assets in 1941. He was home for Christmas, but did not stay much longer. When he was demo-bilised at Wolseley Barracks in London, Ontario on 23 January 1946, he had already moved on.

A century ago, understanding of the psychological after-effects of combat was so poor it was not uncommon for the 'nervous shock' suffered by troops involved in the trench warfare during the First World War to be interpreted as cowardice, for which some were condemned to face a firing squad. Even in more recent times, the authorities have been most reluctant to concede that combatants in the Gulf Wars suffered psychological dysfunction such as post-traumatic stress disorder. For troops of my father's generation, there was also little or no provision for those who needed help with such mental health problems. In Britain, it was at least recognised that some of its armed forces personnel, brutalised by their service experience, needed help with their re-socialisation. A Civilian Resettlement Unit was established for that purpose in Egham, Surrey.

However, for the most part, psychological disorders experienced by Second World War veterans were treated with official indifference or denial. Some ex-servicemen were helped with vocational training, like my adoptive father, who attended a government training centre in Waddon, South London to train as a glazier. But little else was on offer. In consequence, for the majority of ex-servicemen, help with their adjustment to 'Civvy Street' was found informally in the often unspoken support and solidarity of Remembrance Day parades, occasional reunions with former comrades, or at local Legion branches. From my childhood, I have a clear memory of the Sunday lunchtime 'parades' of First World War veterans in their invalid carriages and the younger generation of Second World War men, often kitted out in their brown or navy blue pin-stripe 'demob' suits, making their way to the Legion, and the camaraderie it provided away from their families and everyday lives.

On my father's return to Canada, his membership of the Royal Canadian Legion became a life-long anchoring point. In common with all but a few of his contemporaries, he said very little about his wartime experience within his family circle, and left no account of any personal involvement he might have had in its terrors and horrors. It was nevertheless plain to his family that his adjustment to civilian life was not achieved without difficulty. When demobilised after four and a half years of service, he was still only twenty-two years old. His stay at his parents' home in Strathroy lasted little more than a month before he decided to move to Petrolia. His younger sister, Aunt Shirley, remembered that throughout his brief stay he had been rather ill at ease, with no friends or peer group in the vicinity to whom he could turn.

Petrolia held three attractions. Two older siblings were already living there; prospects of employment were thought to be better; and it was a more familiar town, where he had paraded after enlisting and where friends and acquaintances lived. Within a very short time, my father found a yet more compelling attraction when he met and married a local girl, Selena Irwin. They were married at the Central United Church Manse in Sarnia on 3 September 1946, just two months before the bride's seventeenth birthday. They set up home in Petrolia, where the first of their two children, Marlene, was born in November 1947.

It took time – around four or five years – for my father to establish himself in settled employment. Before doing so, he drifted from job to job. On arrival in Petrolia, he found a job and a home with his older sister, Coralie (my cousin Beth's mother), helping out during her husband's absence while serving in the army of occupation in Holland and Germany. He also had spells as a deliveryman for Canada Bread and as a bus driver, with his income from those sources supplemented by his earnings from an ice cutting and distribution sideline in which he worked alongside his older brother, Charles Fay, in whose home he had also lodged after his discharge from military service. The turning point occurred in or around 1950, when he secured his first position in the local petrochemical industry, at the Canada Oil plant in Corunna. With no formal educational or vocational qualifications to his name, it is likely that his wartime role in the RCASC Petrol Company was the passport into that industry, in which he worked to retirement from his supervisor's position at Nova Corp, Corunna in 1989.

My half-brother, Michael, was born in 1957. By that time, my father was established in the petrochemical industry, and had started to spend periods of time away from home working in Newfoundland and also in Oakville on the western shore of Lake Ontario. His family was beginning to benefit from a moderately prosperous lifestyle. Cine film footage, recorded on the family's wind-up, 8-millimetre camera, dates from that time. Together with photographs, that footage – which also features my grandparents and other members of the extended family – shows my father at ease, participating in family gatherings and on annual camping holidays at lakeside locations. For me, though, the most emotive scenes capture moments at play with his children in the snow, at the lakeside, in the forest. Those insights into what he had been like as a parent were a source of vicarious childhood experience.

Every family has its setbacks. In the case of my father's family, Michael's death in 1974 was incomparably the most serious in both its immediate impact and longer-term consequences. While no parents cope easily with the loss of a child, reports suggest my father and his wife found that life-shattering event even more difficult to come to terms with than most. I have been told they experienced considerable problems in handling their grief, both individually and as a couple. For a time, my father 'hit the bottle'. There was also a temporary separation, during which his wife moved out of the family home to live on her own in Petrolia.

Eventually, time assuaged the rawness of their grief and they were able to resume their life together. They had the distraction of grandchildren and, later, great grandchildren. Their interest in extending, renovating and refurbishing the homes in which they lived before selling them on was rekindled. They involved themselves in the activities of the Legion in Corunna, where they served terms as President of the Branch and its Auxiliary (women's section), and the Masonic Lodge into which my father had been initiated in 1972. They acquired a cottage on land leased from the Saugeen First Nation on the shore of Lake Huron, where they could retreat or entertain family during summer months. For a time, they also owned a trailer park home near Punta Gorda in Florida, which was often used as a refuge from the harsh excesses of southwestern Ontario's winter weather. Footage of their golden wedding celebration in 1996, in the company of a large circle of family and friends, suggests that earlier upsets had been overcome and their last years together were a time of contentment.

Though they may have more in common with the muted, monochrome tints of a moonlit landscape than a more richly-coloured, textured canvas, the results of my enquiries have provided a picture of my father at different stages of his life, and an outline of the main events, experiences and affiliations from childhood to his later years that shaped the life he led. However, an appreciation of his character and personality proved more elusive, not least because those aspects could only be perceived through a hall of mirrors, the reflections and refractions of others' memories and perceptions. Those limitations could leave room to query the validity of the picture I have formed. But, on balance, I believe that any potential distortion has been minimised by the readiness of those who knew him to describe both strengths and weaknesses, to provide a 'warts and all' account.

The image that emerged from the hall of mirrors was that, generally, my father was an emotionally tight-reined man with an outwardly gruff demeanour, but whose gruffness masked a gregarious, clubbable disposition and a dry, occasionally sardonic sense of humour. His personality seems to have been characterised by inner tensions between his public and private selves, between a need for social acceptance and group membership, and a potentially conflicting desire for privacy and independence, to be – or to be seen to be – his own man.

By all accounts, in outlook and manners he was 'old school', a mix of conservative, chauvinist values and gentlemanly conduct. Since those attributes were forged long before publication of *The Female Eunuch* in 1970, it is not surprising to have learned that his stance remained immune from the changes in gender equality that Germaine Greer's work set in train. For instance, there is no indication that he was persuaded to modify his paternalistic approach to family finance, in which major decisions could often be taken with little or no consultation. Also, at work, he is said to have experienced great difficulty in adjusting his supervisory style when women were recruited to his previously all-male workplace team. The gentlemanly aspects of his conduct and character were never more evident than at the numerous social events to which he escorted his wife and her widowed sisters, at which evenings would be spent dancing with each in turn. (Indeed, dancing seems to have been an enduring passion!) A thoughtful, generous nature was also evident in life-long habits of turning up with small gifts, first for his younger siblings and later for his wife and children, and sharing household chores, especially when his wife was running her own business.

Given my father's limited formal education and lack of recognised qualifications, it was not possible to gauge his intellect. That said, it is my impression that he was a shrewd man, such shrewdness never more evident than in his property dealings, in which time and again his decisions to buy and sell suggested a seemingly prescient grasp of market forces. More generally, it is my impression that he was an active, industrious, pragmatic man, very much more inclined to spend time on tasks in and around his home and garden than on more reflective 'armchair' pursuits. Like my adoptive father, he appears to have been a man who said what he meant, expecting that to be the end of the matter and who was not naturally inclined to debate for its own sake. But he was also a man who thrived on company and who enjoyed socialising with family, friends and associates at the Lodge and Legion. So, though he undoubtedly enjoyed passing the time of day with those who crossed his path, on more serious matters he was more inclined to keep his own counsel.

From the hall of mirrors, there were also glimpses of a possibly darker aspect of my father's character, suggestive of a struggle with past demons, but which – if true – was unspoken. That deeper, darker side appears to have found expression in an addictive trait, hinted in photographs which betray a life-long fondness for his cigarettes and alcohol, and underlined by reports indicating that, for a time, his response to Michael's death had been to 'hit the bottle', with one such incident resulting in a driving disqualification. If so, the causation of that trait, which could have contributed to his comparatively early demise, remains unclear. But to allow hints of a darker side to obscure or outweigh other more positive and engaging attributes could constitute an injustice and a disservice to his memory.

The search for my father involved many twists and turns, and was marked by setbacks and periods of frustration. Even though I found much to admire in the achievements of Project Roots and The Association of Liberation Children, I am convinced that in my case, it wouldn't have helped to have relied on that type of assistance. Given the dependence of such agencies on official channels, I believe that any intervention that might have been made on my behalf is likely to have ended in an unresolved cases file, having hit the buffers of evasion, denial or rejection. It is also my belief, as I learned at a very early stage, that any direct approach made personally to the Canadian authorities would have been similarly doomed to failure. There was no realistic possibility of surmounting the barricades enshrined in Canada's privacy and access to information legislation. In bypassing those obstacles, by pursuing my enquiries informally and without reliance on 'official channels', the approach I adopted has been both vindicated and rewarded by the outcomes achieved.

Having traced my father, I have now seen what he looked like and heard the sound of his voice. I have also learned much about the life he led and his family, and have uncovered hitherto unknown North American ancestral roots. I have now travelled in those forebears' footsteps and, like them, found a new world. And, while regretful that my father and I were fated not to meet, that disappointment has been offset by acceptance and inclusion in his family.

The task of tracing my father was made easier because both his first name and surname, though not rare, were comparatively uncommon. Establishing that we were related might also have been more difficult, but for our strong resemblance. A social anthropologist observing how that likeness was noticed and commented upon, both in meetings with family members and in responses to photographs shared with those who lived more distantly, might have perceived in those encounters and reactions a form of social ritual, akin to the quite commonly-demonstrated behaviour of relatives who examine a newly-born infant for signs of parental likeness. Later, I was to learn that it was not only my Canadian relatives who had spotted such resemblance. Apparently, when I was in my late teens, my maternal aunts had also noticed and remarked on it. If my mother also recognised that likeness, as she most surely must have done, it would seem that she kept her reaction to that 'apparition' to herself.

Although there were abundant reasons for contentment with the results of my quest, there were also issues that still perturbed me. One had its roots in the stark contrast between the spontaneity and warmth of the reaction of my father's family and the collusion of my mother's family in the maintenance of a veil of secrecy about my parentage throughout her lifetime. Why had it been kept secret? What truths lay behind it? Another issue concerned questions of identity. Passing years might have rendered such questions hypothetical. Nevertheless, it was unavoidable that my discoveries would prompt me to wonder whether earlier knowledge of my paternal ancestry, paternity and/or contact with my father during his lifetime would have influenced my own outlook and experience and, if so, how?

10

Maternal Roots

Older generations

Had I not learned about my Anglo-Canadian parentage, the essence of my ancestry, including the eventual intertwining of maternal and paternal lines, would have remained unknown. It is unlikely that the family history bug would have bitten for a different reason. As I have since realised, the family in which I was raised was more inclined to secrecy and cover-up than reminiscence and oral history. There had been little to stir curiosity about my forebears.

Interest in my mother's family history took root between the tracing of my father's name in the 'Last Post' section of the Legion Magazine's website in March 2005 and the first telephone call to my Canadian first cousin Beth a year later. Although it developed into a more substantial undertaking, that interest was first viewed as a practice run to acquire the expertise needed to investigate my father's family background, should the opportunity ever arise.

On my mother's side, my ancestry is East Anglian, in particular from the counties of Cambridgeshire and Norfolk. In retrospect, how little I knew – or, worse, cared to know – about those forebears shames me. Clifford and Bridget (Cornwell) Bray, two of my maternal great grandparents, were still alive during my childhood. But I grew up learning very little about them or their ties to other village families. I merely assumed that some 'aunts' to whom my grandmother introduced me had courtesy titles and not, as I was to find out, distant kinship. The other great grandparents, George and Mary Ann (Ellum, née Wayman) Smith, had passed away long

117

before I was born. I do not recall seeing a single photograph of them before starting these enquiries. The little that was known about them had mostly been garnered from occasional snippets my grandfather passed on in conversation.

In the decade before he passed away in 1980, my grandfather, Arthur George Smith, filled a spiral bound notebook with his 'memories'. That memoir is more a maudlin apologia than a balanced narrative of his life and times. But, despite its short-comings, it remains a valuable source for the light it sheds on his parents' and his own lives and outlook. Those reminiscences include passing mentions of his paternal grandfather and maternal grand-mother, both of whom visited his childhood home, but they do not convey any deeper knowledge or appreciation of his family's history. Had he wished to enquire, he would have found that Burwell's parish registers contain many references to his surname, Smith (alternatively spelt Smithe, Smyth or Smythe), also the name under which my birth was registered. The records go back to 1561–62, soon after the accession of Elizabeth I, with his own ancestral roots clearly traceable back to the last quarter of the seventeenth century.

Although he is not mentioned in my grandfather's memoir, he may have been aware that his great grandfather, James Smith, was a farmer. The 1841 census recorded that James was farming, and the village tithe map and associated records from that time show that he was the tenant of two parcels of the land that was allotted to landowners when the village's open fields were subdivided after an Enclosure Act for Burwell was passed in 1815.

Since they were still alive during his younger years and were mentioned in his memoir, my grandfather was certainly aware that James' sons, Stephen (his grandfather) and William, also spent their working lives as farmers or smallholders, as did his father, George Smith, a son from Stephen's first marriage to Sarah Bridgeman in 1852. Stephen Smith, one of my great great grandfathers, not only farmed as a smallholder but also worked as a mail cart driver both before and after his second marriage in December 1870 to Emma Bloom. An article in *The Cambridge Chronicle* on 25 October 1862 reported that, with effect from 1 January 1863, Burwell's previous postal link with Newmarket was to be replaced by a new route through the villages to Cambridge. Stephen had obviously obtained employment as one of the mail cart drivers.

Stephen's later years were not spent in Burwell, but in London, where three daughters from his second marriage had relocated. In his memoir, my grandfather recalled from childhood that his grandfather had travelled from London for holidays in Burwell. Those memories include occasions when he accompanied him to services held in an evangelist's tent erected in a Sunday school meadow near his home: 'I can see him now singing the hymn "O Lamb of God I come, I come", with tears running down his face.' That reminiscence was followed by a more prosaic recollection about a house leek plant that grew beside his parents' kitchen, from which he picked leaves to squeeze over his grandfather's corns.

My great grandfather, George Smith, was also twice married. In June 1879, he married Sarah Alice Dean, with whom he had four children – Alice Jane (who died when quite young), Bertha, Alfred James and John William, the last three of whom were still living in the village during my childhood. In addition to his smallholding, George had followed in his father's footsteps as a mail cart driver, a role in which – according to my grandfather's memoir – he continued for twenty-six years.

As widower and widow, my great grandparents, George Smith and Mary Ann (Wayman) Ellum, were married at St Giles' Church, Cambridge in April 1899. They were the first members of the Smith family to occupy the family home at the junction between the High Street and Mill Lane, Burwell, where my grandfather was born in April 1900 (and where, in turn, both my mother and I were also born in 1923 and 1944, respectively). Although his maternal grandmother also visited his family home during his childhood, and his mother ensured he met her siblings and his cousins, and although he knew about his mother's first husband, Josiah Ellum, and their son, his half-brother Ernest, it is doubtful he was ever told in any detail about her Wayman family background.

That family's roots were in the villages of Impington and Histon, a few miles north of Cambridge, the birthplaces of my grandfather's maternal great grandparents, John and Elizabeth (Fletcher) Wayman. Because his mother carefully nurtured and guarded her own reputation and strove for respectability, I doubt my grandfather ever learned that, after her husband John's early demise, his great grandmother, Elizabeth, entered a relationship with a man who was eighteen years younger (and who she later married), alongside whom, at the County Quarter Sessions in 1851, she received a custodial sentence. She was sentenced to six months hard labour in the town jail and he was sentenced to transportation, later apparently commuted to ten years imprisonment, for their parts in the theft of a sheep. Nor is it likely that my grandfather was ever informed that his mother and her six siblings were all born out of wedlock, the youngest six, including his mother, from a long-term, common law union between her mother, also named Mary Ann Wayman, and her mother's uncle, Frederick Lewis, into whose home she moved with her first-born son after the demise of his wife.

There can be little doubt that my great grandmother, the younger Mary Ann, had the least auspicious imaginable origin and upbringing. Born to a single parent in a common law union with an older man, it is difficult to perceive her as the same stern, chapel-going mother so evidently adored by my grandfather and the overbearing matriarch who my mother recalled had dominated her childhood home. On a personal level, little is known about her early life. Her birth certificate shows she was born in 1861, her birthplace the Blackamoor Head Yard, Cambridge, the first of three such locations, all located within or on the fringes of the town's red light district, in which she and her siblings were raised.

She was therefore brought up in an impoverished urban environment as depicted in the novels of Charles Dickens and Mrs Elizabeth Gaskell. The (public house) yards of Cambridge in the middle of the nineteenth century, in which those formative years were spent, were focal points for prostitution and crime. Other than Elizabeth Wayman's conviction, it is not known if there was any other family involvement in that nefarious underworld. But the possibility of such an association cannot be lightly dismissed. As local historian, C. Hadley, has pointed out, the Cross Keys Inn building (where the older Mary Ann and several of her children were living in 1881 and 1891), though no longer a public house, still retains in its external architecture: '... carved wooden gargoyles, certain large anatomical features of which leave you in no doubt as to what went on in there!'

Seemingly, Cambridge held few attractions for the younger Mary Ann. Before her twentieth birthday, she had left the town to work as a cook in the household of Mr and Mrs Charles Bayley in Soho Square, London. In 1883, she married Josiah Ellum from Great Shelford, who was then serving as a soldier in the Brigade of Guards. Their son Ernest was born in London in 1888. However, by 1891, they had moved to Cambridge, where Josiah worked as a college kitchen porter before ill health, attributed to his military service, resulted in his death in 1897.

My grandfather's memoir noted that his mother's first husband had been a soldier who, at some time, had served in Egypt. No details are known, but that service could have been in relation to the British occupation of Egypt in 1882 to protect the recently-opened Suez Canal. The memoir noted that his mother made shirts for soldiers and also his pride in having held on to her sewing machine almost ninety years later. (I too remember that sewing machine, which was accorded pride of place in his home beside the living room window and behind his Windsor armchair.)

Thanks to my grandfather's memoir, there is much more information about his parents than is disclosed in official records. His account portrays his father as a 'chapel' man, who regularly attended the Congregational Chapel, just a short distance from his home. George Smith also appears to have been an industrious man who worked as an agricultural labourer and mail cart driver, before developing his smallholding and converting his mailman's job into his own business.

Although my grandfather does not mention his own grandfather

Stephen's employment as a mail cart driver, he does describe aspects of his father's work. It entailed an 18-mile route through the villages to Cambridge, setting off from Burwell at 6.30 p.m. six days a week, with a brief overnight stay before following the route in reverse in order to arrive in Burwell around 6.30 a.m. the next day. The journey, which involved collection and delivery of mail and other goods at post offices along the way, was made in all winds and weathers, and on roads or tracks that bore scant resemblance to modern thoroughfares. At first, he undertook that job as an employee of a Mr Moore from Cambridge, for whom he also broke in the horses used to pull the mail carts. By 1911, though, the route had been divided into two and George Smith, who had become self-employed, won the contracts for both new routes, purchasing one of the two mail carts he needed second-hand and having the other purpose-built.

Earlier, in or around 1906, while still working as a mailman, George Smith entered into a partnership with a Mr Hawkes, the owner of a house and grounds at the junction of High Street and Hall Lane, Burwell. The outbuildings of that property were used to stable their horses, house two cows which provided milk and other dairy products for the Smith household and generally act as a base for their farming activities.

My grandfather's memoir conveys a sense of regret that an early death deprived his father of fuller enjoyment of the fruits of his labours. According to that account, George Smith became ill around 1915 – ill health my grandfather attributed to an earlier accident caused by a horse his father was breaking in for the mail cart, which shied, snapped its backstrap and bolted over a ditch. Seemingly, when he attempted to jump off the cart, his mailman's coat caught on the step entrapping him and causing significant injuries to his ribs. It was my grandfather's belief that, in conjunction with 'worry', those injuries: '... hasten(ed) his end as he died at the age of sixty-three on July 27th 1917.' (He was in fact sixty-one.)

Mary Ann was one of life's 'survivors'. After her husband's death, she lived on for another twenty-one years. She was photographed next to my grandfather at his marriage to Kate Bray, and was well remembered by my mother and her sisters, the children of that union. Accounts suggest she was a domineering, matriarchal figure who, whether inadvertently or by design, cast a long, destructive shadow over her son's marriage, and who ultimately may have contributed more than a little to its eventual breakdown.

Kate Bray was born in Burwell in 1901, the third of six children from the marriage of Clifford and Bridget (Cornwell) Bray. Although neither she nor her husband survived to see more recent developments in new technologies, they lived through two world wars and the intervening years of economic depression, during which their four daughters were born. They were nevertheless witnesses to significant developments in science, engineering, technology and communications – motor vehicles superseding horse-drawn transport; air and space travel from the Wright brothers' inaugural manned flight to the first moon landing; the invention and proliferation of radio, film and television; the creation and use of atomic weapons; and the wider impact of such developments on everyday life and society.

Compared to Smith forebears, who had remained firmly rooted in Burwell for generations, my grandmother's ancestors were more geographically mobile. From at least the late eighteenth century onwards, her paternal forebears' roots were in Norfolk, in particular in and around the town of King's Lynn and in the villages that encircle the royal estate at Sandringham. In the time of her great grandparents, Henry and Ann (Benstead) Bray, King's Lynn was still a flourishing east coast port. Henry Bray and his father John before him both worked in the town's docks as coal porters.

Henry's son, Henry William Bray and his wife Lucy Whall, my great great grandparents, were born and raised in King's Lynn, where Henry William trained as a cabinet maker. It was the beginning of an itinerant lifestyle in which his work took him and his family to Hull, (where my great grandfather, Clifford Bray, was born in 1877) and back to King's Lynn, before other periods of residence in Newmarket and Burwell, where Lucy died in 1896. The parish record of Henry William's death in 1908 disclosed that his last days were spent in the Exning Union, the local workhouse, suggesting that, like his mother Ann (Benstead) Bray, who spent her later years on parish relief in King's Lynn, his life ended in destitution.

Some of Kate Bray's maternal forebears also had Norfolk roots. Her great grandfather, George Bloom and his parents were also from King's Lynn, although their family's work as livestock dealers and butchers took them to Carlton, on the border between Cambridgeshire and Suffolk, before they too ended their days in Burwell. In the course of his business travels, George Bloom met and married Elizabeth Anderson from Therfield in Hertfordshire. Their oldest daughter, Catharine, went on to marry Henry Cornwell, a drover and livestock dealer from Fordham, Burwell's neighbouring village. My great grandmother, Bridget, born in 1876, was the youngest of Henry and Catharine's six children.

Clifford and Bridget (Cornwell) Bray, my other maternal great grandparents, were the first of my mother's forebears of whom I have any memory. As a child, I was a frequent visitor to their home, a small, semi-detached, two-bedroom bungalow, which at first lacked electricity and was lit by oil lamps. One of my errands was to take the accumulator that powered their wireless set to a local shop for recharging. Thinking back to that time, my earliest school years, I can still recall the spicy aroma of my great grandmother's fruit cakes, and have a very clear image of my great grandfather seated in his wooden armchair alongside the range, with his pipe rack and cherry wood pipes, all crafted by his own hands, within easy reach. I also remember his last years at home, after his wife's death in 1952, when he became blind and bedridden, and was nursed by my grandmother for several years before he went into residential care, where he passed away in 1964.

My great grandparents were married at Burwell's parish church in August 1896. The marriage certificate records that, like his father before him, Clifford had trained as a carpenter. Bridget was merely described as a spinster, with no occupation mentioned. Presumably for reasons of work, in the late 1890s, with his father and younger brother 'in tow', Clifford and Bridget moved to Pleasley, a small village on the Nottinghamshire-Derbyshire border. The 1901 census recorded them as living there with two daughters, Agnes and Charlotte Edith. Both Clifford and his father were working as joiner/carpenters.

My great grandparents were at different addresses in Burwell and London in 1911, his employment as a carpenter in the building trade having once again taken my great grandfather from the village. During the intervening years, another daughter and two sons had been born. They were my maternal grandmother, Kate, Clifford and James. A third son, Walter Ernest, followed midway through the First World War. While my great grandfather continued to work as and when opportunities arose through the years of the general strike and the depression that followed in the wake of the 1929 Wall Street crash, my great grandmother devoted much of her spare time to the parish church, through her longstanding membership of the Mothers' Union and as one of the parishioners on its cleaning rosters.

Arthur George and Kate (Bray) Smith

A year after the birth of my maternal grandfather, Arthur George, George and Mary Ann Smith had a second son, Frederick, who sadly survived for no more than a few days. My grandfather, therefore, was their only (surviving) child. Though for a time he was raised alongside Ernest and John William, sons from, respectively, his mother's and father's first marriages (his other older half-siblings, Bertha and Alfred James, having moved on), he would appear to have received a favoured, if not thoroughly pampered, upbringing. That dotage was reciprocated. His memoir left no doubt that, throughout his life, his parents were held in much higher esteem than all others, including his wife and children. A hallmark of emotional immaturity, that character flaw found expression in a life led as an unreconstructed 'mother's boy'.

125

My grandfather's reminiscences certainly suggest that his mother, the family's driving force, was determined to ensure his childhood would not be touched by the disadvantages that had attended her own upbringing in Cambridge. Even if allowance is made for a measure of 'rose tint' in those recollections, it is evident that Mary Ann Smith was prepared to work hard to ensure her family's respectability and prosperity. Apart from her homemaking responsibilities, she served the community by attending births, laying out the dead, nursing the sick and taking in the laundry of those who could no longer cope with it themselves.

Whether or not George Smith regularly attended chapel before his second marriage is unclear, although he and Mary Ann became regular worshippers at the Congregational Chapel thereafter. My grandfather not only accompanied them to the two Sunday services, but also attended the Sunday school and midweek Christian Endeavour meetings with his mother. Almost certainly, it was also Mary Ann's influence that was responsible for the efforts my great grandfather made to build up his smallholding interests and, when the opportunity arose, to convert his mail cart-driving job into self-employment.

In my grandfather's case, Mary Ann's ambitions were expressed in two main ways. The first, no doubt reflecting her own lack of formal schooling and illiteracy, was the importance she attached to his education. He was sent to school around the age of three years and, once able to read and write, was encouraged to become his mother's reader of newspapers and correspondence and scribe, although the age from which he performed those tasks is not known. He was also encouraged to save the money he earned from errands and other tasks at home and on the smallholding, a habit that was, at least in part, the foundation of the reputation he acquired later in life for penny-pinching thrift – for having 'long pockets'.

But it was not all work and no play. His parents entertained friends and family, the latter including my great great grandfather Stephen, who was then living in London and my great great grandmother, the older Mary Ann Wayman, who was then living in

126

Cambridge with her youngest daughter, Elizabeth Adams. His mother also ensured that my grandfather spent holidays with her sisters' children in Cambridge, in particular the Hill and Adams families. He was particularly fond of his uncle Bill Adams, a porter at Trinity College, who taught him the rudiments of boxing and wrestling. In addition, there were theatre visits made with his mother and participation in the village's feast days and public holidays. The latter were marked by parades that would pass in front of his home on High Street, and such associated activities as swimming in the Lode, and outings on horse-drawn barges along the river.

When he was eleven, my grandfather transferred to the Boys School at the Guildhall, adjacent to the parish church. He attended that school for another three years, his attendance having been extended for one year to compensate for two long absences during which, contrary to the common practice of 'isolation' in the local fever hospital, his mother nursed him at home through bouts of scarlet fever in 1905 and 1912.

On leaving school in 1914, he obtained his first job as a butcher's boy. His employer was his half-sister Bertha's husband, John Bateman. He worked for John until his father was taken ill in 1915, when he commenced a year's employment as a postman. In his memoir, my grandfather recalled that, around that time (most probably in 1916), some two years after the onset of the First World War, his patriotism led him to answer the national call to arms. With three of his Cambridge cousins, two of William and Harriet (Wayman) Hill's sons and Herbert William Adams, the son of his favoured Uncle Bill and Aunt Elizabeth, he tried to enlist in the Cambridgeshire Regiment. The two Hill brothers were killed in action in France soon after their arrival in the trenches, and his other cousin, Herbert, who later was the best man at his wedding, was invalided out after suffering a leg wound. But my grandfather, who was two or three years younger, never saw action. His father intervened, informing the authorities that his son was under age for military service, and secured his return home.

That would have been during the year before his father's death in

July 1917. In his will, George Smith left everything to his wife, entreating his son to take care of his mother, a responsibility that was discharged to the detriment of all other family obligations. It was from that date that my grandfather commenced self-employment. I have never forgotten his account of his first challenge, bringing in that year's harvest, a task that had to be undertaken without the benefit of either machinery or the funds to hire help. Single-handedly, he had to scythe, bind sheaves, stook, cart and stack the harvest by hand until, in his rather graphic description: '... the sweat ran down my arse.'

While I know those tasks were performed on 5 of the 7 acres on Reach Road, which remain in the family's ownership at the time of writing, I am less sure whether he was obliged to harvest other fields as well. From the memoir, it is apparent that the land he inherited was in itself not enough to rely upon for a living. Consequently, as with his father before him, his striving for self-sufficiency made it necessary to take on additional work using the horses his father had needed for his smallholding and the mail carts.

Having acquired knowledge of horses and horsemanship from his father, that expertise was put to effective use over the next decade, during which my grandfather found numerous ways in which to turn a penny. In addition to ploughing his own land, he subcontracted to plough allotments throughout the village and also to undertake the double-depth ploughing needed to prepare ground for the planting of orchards. He inherited or acquired a landau. It was used occasionally for family outings, but mainly as a 'taxi' to convey race-goers between Newmarket station, the racecourse and their local hotel accommodation. It proved to be a lucrative sideline until the general strike in 1926, after which the race-goers turned to buses and other forms of motor transport.

Other work came from hiring out his services as a carter, transporting various loads to and from the village. The list of goods carried included grain, coal, coke, sand and gravel, straw for the racing stables, fruit and vegetables, livestock, and the ashes and sewage – the 'midnight soil' – cleared annually from the earth closets of the village alms houses, taken as fertiliser for his land. He also acquired a hearse, used for local funerals, when the landau could also be pressed into service to convey mourners. But that business also declined after the introduction of motorised hearses. Before that development, the hearse had also been used from time to time to convey the remains of patients who had died in the isolation hospital between Exning and Fordham – patients with infectious diseases like scarlet fever and diphtheria, who he had earlier conveyed from their homes in surrounding villages to the hospital in its fever van.

It is probable that these were examples of a range of tasks performed at different times to supplement income from the smallholding. Certainly, within a short time of his father's death, my grandfather was on the lookout for more land to farm, and in 1919 was able to secure a five-year lease on a five-acre field across the road from the railway station. Thus, in the early 1920s, when he courted my grandmother, it is likely he was considered to be a very eligible bachelor, not simply for his industry and potential, but also his looks (for, when attired in his horseman's breeches, leggings, apron and bowler hat, he must have cut quite a dash), particularly since the pool of marriageable men had been severely depleted by the carnage of the First World War.

Much less is known about my grandmother, Kate Bray's childhood. She did not leave a memoir and it is a part of her life about which she said very little. She was born after her parents returned to the village from Pleasley, Derbyshire, where her father's work had taken the family. She spent her childhood in the village and attended the local girls' school, leaving on the eve of the First World War. The impression gained from what little she did say about her early years is that she was raised in a household in which her mother, with support from her own mother and maternal aunts (the Cornwells), were the main source of stability, her father's work as a carpenter occasioning frequent and sometimes prolonged absences. It would also seem that while not living in a state of destitution – it is doubtful that Cornwell relatives would have tolerated that – the Bray family's circumstances were impoverished. If that were not so, it is unlikely that her grandfather, Henry William Bray, would have been admitted to the local workhouse toward the end of his life, or that in 1911 my grandmother, her mother and siblings were found to be living in a household headed by (and so under the watchful and caring eye of) her grandmother Catharine Cornwell.

Shortly after that date, my grandmother's oldest sister, Agnes, left home to work in domestic service. Her other sister, Edith, followed soon after. That left my grandmother to help her mother with the house and upbringing of two younger brothers, Clifford and James, and possibly also the third, Walter Ernest, after his birth in 1916. Caring for children became a defining feature of her life. For example, she first encountered my grandfather around 1915, when he was working in his first job as a butcher's boy for John Bateman and when she was employed to help look after the Batemans' children. After that, she followed her older sisters into service in Cambridge. (When I left home to attend university, I inherited the small metal trunk into which her personal belongings had been packed for that purpose almost fifty years earlier.)

There is no record of how long my grandmother spent in service, or the circumstances in which she and my grandfather conducted the courtship leading to their marriage in the parish church in Burwell in March 1923. After the ceremony, the bride, groom and their guests assembled for a group photograph. It is a telling record for the light it seems to shed on family dynamics, not only on that day, but also into the future. On the bride's side, guests included her parents, Clifford and Bridget (Cornwell) Bray, and her five siblings. They also included her maternal aunts Harriet (Cornwell) Harling, Harriet's husband Edgar and two daughters, one of whom, Lilian, was a bridesmaid, and Charlotte (Cornwell) Reeve, Charlotte's husband Robert and their son Harry. The groom's support included his mother Mary Ann and her younger sister Elizabeth (Wayman) Adams and her husband, William, their two daughters and their son, Herbert, who was best man. In contrast, not one of my grandfather's half-siblings, the offspring of George Smith's first marriage, was present. Reasons for their absence are open to speculation. But it cannot be discounted either that their father's second wife had not met with their approval (perhaps they were aware of the Wayman family's history and reputation) or that Mary Ann had acted to distance her husband from his first family. It would certainly be surprising if George Smith's will, which made no provision whatsoever for the children from his first marriage, had not engendered a sense of grievance.

The other striking feature of the wedding party photograph is the absence of any suggestion of a joyous occasion. In particular, though there is no contact between the bride and groom, there is a strong hint that the camera caught the groom reaching for or holding his mother's hand. Significantly, it was not a white wedding. It was, rather, a 'shotgun' union, from which the first child was born four months later. Quite possibly, it was a marriage that went ahead against the bridegroom's mother's wishes, the unplanned pregnancy having scotched any aspiration she might have entertained for her son to secure a better match.

There was no honeymoon. On her wedding night, the bride moved into her mother-in-law's home, and into the shadow under which the next fifteen years would be spent. During that time, their four daughters – Margaret Kate, Ellen Mary, Doreen May Elizabeth and Georgina – were born and raised under my great grandmother's sternly watchful sway.

Confronted by a loss of income as motorised transport – lorries, taxis, buses, ambulances, hearses – gradually supplanted the horse-drawn business activities on which he previously relied, and with a young family to support, my grandfather turned his hand to building up his smallholding, purchasing or leasing fields and meadows in different locations around the village. In 1927, he started to build a yard with stabling for his horses, but was obliged to give that up through shortage of funds, blaming the worsening economic climate. Undeterred, he struggled on, and two years later acquired land alongside Reach Road, opposite the field he harvested after his father's death and formerly part of the village sheep walk, where he built the yard that became the base for his subsequent farming activities, and that was still in his ownership when he died.

His memoir makes numerous references to the hardship he endured throughout the economic depression of the 1930s, though to my mother's recollection the family never went hungry. Nevertheless, any memories she might have had of a happy childhood seemed few and far between. If my grandparents' marriage ever started with romance, it soon disintegrated. My great grandmother remained domineering and, it is believed, disapproving. My grandfather became more and more frustrated by his wife's failure to produce a son and heir. And my great grandmother's final and most destructive gesture was to sow poisonous seeds of doubt in her son's mind about his wife's fidelity.

Too young to do his patriotic duty during the First World War, and too old to enlist in 1939, my grandfather spent the Second World War contributing to the feeding of the nation and serving as an Air Raid Patrol warden. My own memories of him date from the post-war years. He was then in his prime, farming around sixty acres of arable land, half owned and half leased, fattening twenty bullocks a year, breeding his own pigs and poultry, and employing two or three farm labourers at any given time.

But he was not a progressive farmer and was the last in the village to convert from horse to tractor power. He acquired a sobriquet – 'the midnight farmer'. It was a reflection of his inability to keep to the pattern of early-rising characteristic of almost every agricultural worker and, hence, the need he had from time to time to work on into the twilight hours or sometimes later. I imagine his reluctance to face the day was a habit acquired from his father, who was regularly away overnight with the mail cart and would rest on his return home before attending to his smallholder duties. One of my earliest memories is of my grandfather's men, having fed the livestock and groomed the horses that were stabled alongside his home, standing idly in the yard waiting for him to finish his breakfast and issue their orders for the day.

If anything was ever done to repair the damage to my grandparents' marriage, it did not succeed. Their relationship was not helped by my grandfather's refusal to allow his wife any say in household finances or to take any steps to modernise their home. He also became involved in a supposedly platonic relationship with a lady who had arrived in the village as a Land Army girl and who stayed on after the war. She was always available to help with the harvest by driving one of the tractors. It must have been particularly galling for my grandmother to meet her when delivering refreshments for those who were involved in the harvesting. Matters came to a head in 1952 amidst allegations and counter-allegations of possibly imagined infidelities, when my grandmother and her youngest daughter (Georgina) arrived home one evening to find themselves locked out of their family home. Though my grandparents never divorced, the breakdown was irretrievable, and they subsequently led wholly separate lives.

After their 'eviction', my grandmother and my aunt moved into my family home until Georgina married and my grandmother moved into her rapidly-ailing father's home, where she looked after him during his final years. Without any other support, she relied on babysitting to provide a modest income which, given her warm and generous nature, she was always willing to share. Although I had no inkling of her reasons for doing so, looking back, I now realise that I was particularly favoured, and was the frequent recipient of a bar of chocolate, a packet of mints or a threepenny bit to spend on sweets. Since finding out about my paternity, it has become clear to me why she acted as a guardian angel throughout my childhood, unafraid to intervene if she thought my adoptive father's attempts to discipline me were too heavy-handed, however well deserved those punishments might have been.

The extent of that protectiveness was also apparent after my grandmother's death in 1965, when her possessions were found to include a chest of drawers crammed with discarded handbags, the contents of which included an assortment of pen knives, sheath knives, catapults, fishing hooks and Dinky racing cars (whose axles had been meticulously oiled to ensure fast performance on the playground or in the streets where they were raced) which I had written off as mislaid, lost or even stolen. All had been surreptitiously confiscated to keep me out of harm's way. Though those items were never returned to their 'lawful owner', I did inherit a talismanic coin, a farthing minted in the year of my birth, which my grandmother had kept in her purse and which, superstitiously, has since had a place in my wallet.

I do not recall my grandmother having a bad word to say about anyone, including the husband from whom she separated or the mother-in-law who overshadowed and almost certainly blighted her marriage. The upset and ill will she must have experienced were never outwardly shown or shared. Her memory, reflecting the esteem in which she was – and is still – held, lives on in the numerous Kates and Katies among her descendants.

In 1965, the year my grandmother passed away, my grandfather reached pensionable age. Following a contentious exchange with the Inland Revenue over the extent to which taxation of his farming income could offset the value of the old age pension to which he was entitled, he declined to apply for that pension. Instead, despite increasing disability arising from a tractor accident, he soldiered on. By 1969, though, having already given up pig rearing and the keeping of poultry, he was obliged to give up the fattening of the stall-fed, cross-bred, Hereford-Black Angus bullocks he tended to favour. Throughout the next decade, during which he drew his state pension, he became progressively less able to perform all other tasks except those requiring the use of a tractor. By then, my own visits to the village had become quite infrequent, and opportunities to meet my grandfather were few. When I did see him, though, the aging process was clearly evident in his increasingly stooped posture and reliance on a walking stick for support, although his fiercely independent spirit, fired by political beliefs which positioned him to the right of the Conservative party, was undiminished.

Two years before my grandfather's death, I received a message that he wished to see me. While unsure of the reason for that summons, I thought it might have something to do with his plans for the eventual disposal of his estate, possibly a request to act as an executor. But, when we met, there was no such discussion and no mention of any other topic of significance. Although it will always be a matter of conjecture, with hindsight I have come to believe his request to see me had a different purpose, that it was his intention – his duty, as he perceived it – to inform me about my paternity. In the event, there was no such discussion. I had arrived to see him in the company of my wife, whose presence might have persuaded him to refrain from broaching that topic. We made our farewells, having sampled his wheat wine, but none the wiser about the reason for his summons.

After a mercifully short period of inpatient treatment (he would have detested the associated dependency), Arthur George Smith passed away in 1980. His memoir leaves little room to doubt that his last years were spent as a lonely, embittered, albeit still feisty man, estranged from his family, still railing about past battles lost or won, and still under his parents' – in particular his mother's – spell.

His memoir painted an idyllic picture of not only his parents, but also his childhood home. It described its veranda and shuttered windows, the uninterrupted views from its upper storey, and the jasmine, lavender, hollyhocks, roses and grapevine in the garden. It recalled the copper in which his father brewed beer for the harvest, his mother's sewing machine and her box mangle, which he used to turn for neighbours in return for contributions to his money box. But what the memoir failed to disclose was the extent to which the property and its fittings and furnishings were in all essentials unchanged from the time of his mother's death in 1938 and, hence, the shabby, Havisham-esque setting in which it was written. Thus, when he died, the property still had an electricity supply to two ground floor rooms only; no heating other than a paraffin stove and the once regularly black-leaded range in the living room; no internal plumbing, water being drawn from a well close to the back door; and lavatory facilities provided by, most probably, the very last earth closet to remain in use in the county. Items removed from that crumbling, matriarchal shrine before its sale and substantial reno-vation included the totemic sewing machine and mangle, and the piano, card table and other items with which his mother had furnished the front parlour. They also included dairy equipment which had not been used for around forty years; the progressively misshapen, ground down, bone-handled cutlery he had used from his childhood; and many other objects and items of furniture my grandmother had never been allowed to remove or replace during their time together.

Regrettably, my grandfather's personal affairs were left in no tidier shape. After his death, his daughters were drawn into a lawsuit of Jarndycean proportions. A former employee, who appears to have insinuated himself into the role of 'adopted son and heir', contested the will. Eventually, after many years of slow, grinding litigation, from which the lawyers undoubtedly profited, he succeeded in securing a negotiated settlement that awarded him part of the estate.

All things considered, my grandfather had only himself to blame for the life he led and the sadness and loneliness that dogged his middle and later years. In almost every respect, he was the author of his own misfortune.

11

Secrecy, Truth, and Identity

A closely guarded secret

On the day of my birth, Max Clements was on the south coast of England, where the 4th Canadian Armoured Division was preparing to cross the Channel to play its part in the allied invasion of Normandy. On the same date, Frederick Cornes, the man who was to become my adoptive father, was on the northeastern frontier of India. He had enlisted in the Territorial Army in London soon after his seventeenth birthday in March 1939, before war was declared. He was amongst the first of those reserve forces to be drafted into the regular army, in his case into the Royal Army Signal Corps (RASC). He was posted overseas in 1942, and had arrived in India after an enforced sojourn in Durban, South Africa (to where the troop ship on which he sailed needed to be towed for repairs, having broken down and been left adrift of the convoy) and a subsequent tour of duty in Iraq.

In India, his RASC unit, in which he was mainly deployed as a driver, was attached to a medium artillery regiment, which advanced into Burma. Having mustered on the Manipur Plain, the regiment passed between the battlegrounds of Imphal and Kohima just a few weeks after the hard-fought and bloody actions there halted the Japanese advance and turned the tide of the war in the Far East. In the weeks and months that followed, he was involved in a crossing of the Chindwin River and an onward advance to the Irrawaddy, during which he and his comrades confronted enemy troops in a series of set-piece jungle warfare and vicious guerrilla rearguard actions as the Japanese army was progressively driven southward in retreat.

During our weekly Sunday morning telephone calls in his later years, he recalled passing Mandalay under fire and that his own personal involvement in hostilities ceased when on the road to Prome, midway between Mandalay and Rangoon. From there, he was airlifted from Magwe Airfield to Chittagong, and was eventually repatriated from India to England, physically unharmed but undoubtedly psychologically scarred, the legacy of which was marked by a lifetime of periodic psychosomatic illness. He disembarked from his troop ship around the time of his twenty-fourth birthday in March 1946.

My mother and adoptive father had met when he was stationed near Burwell before he was posted overseas. He recalled they were sweethearts, and that is how he continued to think about her throughout his time overseas. However, literacy was never his strong point and it appears there was little, possibly no communication between them during that period of almost four years. Certainly, he had not been informed about the cuckoo in the nest. Following some contact between the two families, his family had only belatedly been informed about my birth. He was not told about it until he returned to his home in southwest London. Not surprisingly, his reaction was one of shock and betrayal. Nevertheless, after consideration and discussion with members of his family, he decided to visit my mother at her home in Cambridgeshire.

According to his account, the woman he met that day was not the carefree sweetheart he had left behind in 1942. Rather, he found her to be 'a bag of nerves, a physical wreck', with substantial hair loss and generally in an acutely anxious state. The story told was that she had suffered a nervous breakdown. He was also informed that my birth had resulted from an act of rape by a member of overseas forces and that my mother's poor state of health, mentally and physically, was a direct outcome of that sexual assault and its all-too-evident consequences. (When information about my parentage was first disclosed to me after my mother's demise, I received a similar

138

account. It was extremely hard to digest, to come to terms with. On the grounds that some stones are best left unturned, it was the main reason why I made no effort to trace my biological father for another four years.)

Although little is known about what actually took place, the first meeting, their reunion, must have been very harrowing for both parties. All that my adoptive father could be persuaded to say about that inevitably testing encounter was that eventually his initial anger and loathing were overtaken by other concerns for my mother's welfare. She was after all still the sweetheart for whom he had carried a torch during his years of overseas service. It was characteristic of both his love for my mother and the strong sense of duty that marked his entire life that he opted for forgiveness and reconciliation, to let bygones be bygones, and hence to resume their relationship, part of which would entail assuming some responsibility for my upbringing.

They married a few months later, in July 1946, and my half-sister Maggie, their only child together, was born the following year. Before her birth, they lived with my grandparents, with my adoptive father briefly employed as a labourer on my grandfather's farm. However, relationships were strained, largely because my grandfather seemed to find almost endless fault with his son-in-law's 'city' ways and because they could not agree about the proportion of the weekly wage to be deducted for his keep. Those tensions abated with a move to my adoptive father's family home in Streatham. It was a move that allowed him to attend a government vocational training scheme for ex-servicemen, on which he trained as a glazier. On its completion, our family moved back to Burwell to occupy a newly-built council house, the childhood home in which Maggie and I were raised as brother and sister.

My recollection of that childhood home is that, while it was characterised by industry, support and sacrifice, generally its emotional tone was shallow, sometimes lacking warmth. Overt displays of affection were few and far between. Shared father-son activities were a rarity. However, both parents worked hard to feed and clothe

the family, with little or nothing to spare for extras or luxuries. Consequently, for example, family holidays were limited to occasional day trips to the seaside or short stays with relatives in London or Nottinghamshire.

Though my adoptive father first found employment as a glazier, he gave that up quite soon to commence a series of generally low paid, unskilled or partly-skilled manual jobs, some of which made use of his army training as a driver. My mother also contributed to household income through a succession of domestic cleaning jobs and factory work. Together, partly because he was the type of man who was willing to come home with an unopened pay packet, from which he received a small weekly allowance (his 'cigarette money'), and partly through her skill in managing the household's finances on a budget which only barely kept the family above the poverty line, they created a home that was gradually furnished with a washing machine, refrigerator, television set and other consumer durable trappings of a 1950s lifestyle.

As for my experience of that family home, which was frequently populated by visiting relatives, the overriding feeling that springs to mind in retrospect is a sense of semi-detachment. For all the support he dutifully provided throughout my childhood and adolescence, it cannot be said that my adoptive father and I then enjoyed a particularly close relationship. Indeed, the legal adoption was a delayed affair. It might never have happened but for the requirement a few months before my fourteenth birthday to produce a copy of my birth certificate in connection with a passport application needed for a school trip to Switzerland. It must have set the cat amongst the pigeons, because the only document in the family's possession was the one issued after I was born, which (I now know) bore my birth name, Paul Smith, rather than the name by which I had always been known, at least from earliest school days onwards.

The matter was resolved by appropriate proceedings in the local juvenile court. However, to this day, I have no recollection from those proceedings that I was told any more about the outcome than that I had been formally adopted by the man upon whom I had always looked as my father. I do recall a long wait alone in a room at the Shire Hall in Cambridge, where the hearing was held, before being summoned into the court for no more than three or four minutes toward the end of its deliberations. But I have no memory whatsoever from the ensuing words addressed to me of any reference to the existence of another 'biological' parent. If such information had been provided, there is little doubt that questions about that man's identity would have followed. I can only assume that the court was persuaded to remain silent because of what it had been told about the alleged criminal circumstances of my conception.

Looking back, there is also a sense that my mother, perhaps mindful of past events, also maintained a measure of emotional distance. In any event, whilst, almost invariably, our family meals were shared occasions, other activities in which most families participate together were few and far between. It was also a home with few books and little encouragement of debate or discussion, mainly because my adoptive father was a man who said what he meant and meant what he said, leaving little or no scope to talk anything over. To attempt to do so was to be regarded as being unduly argumentative, as challenging parental authority.

It was only when I reached my twenties that I began to appreciate that a different tactic was needed, and our relationship improved thereafter. Beforehand, from the age of eight or nine to around fifteen years, my response to that environment had been to 'run wild'. In those days, of course, children enjoyed much greater freedom. I used mine to spend as much time as possible away from home, roaming the village streets, fields, hedgerows and riverbanks, frequently getting into mischief and, in one or two instances, engaging in acts of petty delinquency. (In hindsight, none was more pleasing than the adaptation of my sister's butterfly net with the insertion of a razor blade which enabled me to reach the higher branches of fruit trees in the village orchards when 'scrumping'.) When not so engaged, the main attraction was sport, with many hours spent on the football field, cycling and fishing, although I cannot recall a single sporting event in which I took part that my parents attended as spectators.

Parental care and concern were not absent, but generally expressed in other ways, not least through the many sacrifices made to support my education, an opportunity my mother strongly endorsed because she keenly felt she had been deprived of a similar chance. For instance, there was their response to the news in 1955 that I had passed the eleven plus examination, giving me the opportunity to attend the local grammar school. That afternoon, my junior school class had been playing a game of rounders on a nearby Sunday school meadow. When the game was over and it was time to go home, the headmistress, 'Fanny' Carter, instructed me to return to school and wait for her there. After waiting around fifteen minutes without any sign of her appearance, and thinking I had been found out over some act of mischief, or worse, I decided to make good my escape... only to be caught at the school gate and unceremoniously led back inside held by the ear. Once there and having received a scolding for my errant behaviour, I was informed about the examination success and given the relevant paperwork for my parents to sign, confirming that the offer of the grammar school place would be accepted. I was then sent home with the instruction to tell them that they should not concern themselves about the expense involved because they would be eligible to receive financial assistance from the county.

It was very much in keeping with my adoptive father's sense of responsibility (not to mention pride) that the offer of charitable assistance was politely declined. My uniform and other items needed to take up the place were purchased from funds he earned from taking on a second, demeaning, piecework job in which he was set the task of dismantling the barbed wire perimeter fencing around a recently-vacated camp for displaced persons, before cutting it into short lengths and compressing them into forty-gallon oil drums.

Six years later, a similar sacrifice was made. On that occasion, aged seventeen and having left school a year earlier to take up a clerical position in the Civil Service, but having seen the error of my ways, I sought his support for a decision I had made to return to school to pursue the sixth form studies that hopefully would enable me to gain a university place. In that case too, his support was unstinting. Although part-time and holiday jobs enabled me to remain partly independent, I was reliant on him and my mother for the other support needed during the two years that were then spent back in full-time secondary education.

Despite such support, for which I shall always be indebted, the overarching pattern of my boyhood experience – with much of the interaction with my parents throughout my childhood and early adolescent years centred on parental discipline – could suggest that I missed out on much of the warmth and closeness of a more typical father-son relationship. But it did not always remain so, especially after the births of my daughters and, in turn, their children, with whom spontaneous bridges of affection were built in his roles of grandfather and great grandfather. Those inter-generational ties also provided a foundation for improvement of our own relationship, the more so after my mother's death.

The bond was finally cemented one Sunday morning when, prompted by the discoveries that were then emerging from my family history research, but without disclosing the nature of those findings, I admitted to him how remiss I had been in not formally acknowledging and thanking him as fulsomely as I should have done for all the support he had provided during my younger years. His response was not immediate, but as soon as we were back in touch the following week, obviously having mulled matters over, his first words were to acknowledge what had been said in our previous conversation and to express his regret over various incidents in which he now considered his approach might have been too over-bearing. The most amusing – albeit a most serious source of friction at the time – was his insistence that boys should not be allowed to wear long trousers before their fourteenth birthday. That arbitrary 'ruling' was a particular source of annoyance and embarrassment, because it meant that he expected me to wear short trousers when going out on post-match Saturday evening excursions to

Newmarket with the village football team, Burwell Swifts, for whom I was regularly selected to play. He had not been aware that his 'ruling' had been circumvented with the connivance of my grandmother, who purchased long trousers that were then kept in an outhouse, to be furtively donned after leaving the house and taken off before re-entering my home in the 'officially approved' clothing.

Truth Revealed

I do not, and now never will, know exactly what my adoptive father was told about the alleged rapist. He may not even have been told his name. Certainly, to tell him more than that is likely to have invited other questions, the answers to which my mother would have been most reluctant to provide. What was clear, over sixty years later when we discussed the circumstances that resulted in my conception, was that his sense of outrage and withering contempt was undiminished. But whether or not those strong emotions were justified is a different matter. Other lines of enquiry clearly suggested that he, who was so relieved after my mother's passing that there would be 'no more damned secrets', had also been duped by a web of secrecy woven and maintained over the years by my mother, with the complicity of her family.

The evidence to support this theory came from several different strands of information about the thirty-month gap between my conception and my adoptive father's homecoming. First and foremost, there is the issue of the alleged rape. If such a serious, violent offence had been committed, it might be expected that no time would have been lost in reporting it to the local police who would undoubtedly have contacted the Canadian military authorities. The alleged perpetrator's identity was known and he was still stationed locally. Almost certainly, a formal complaint would have led to an arrest and trial before an English civil court. Canadian army historical records leave no doubt about the co-operation maintained between military and civil authorities over such matters.

But no evidence has been traced to indicate that any formal complaint was made. Rather, it would appear, my grandparents only found out much later, after my mother's pregnancy was confirmed and my biological father had left the area with the rest of the 4th Canadian Armoured Division. So it is more likely that my grandfather's reported contact with the Canadian authorities was made at that later time, as an angry father seeking to 'hunt down' the young man responsible for his daughter's pregnancy.

That interpretation of events fits more readily with other information. It may explain why I was told that my mother might have retained some mementos of her relationship with my father, 'the dancing partner', and also why my aunts had no difficulty in identifying him from the photograph received from Canada at an early stage of my enquiries. Evidently, he was no stranger to the Smith family. It may also explain two more recent disclosures.

The first is that during his time in England my father sent a letter to his mother in which he informed her that he had become engaged. Apparently, the letter included sufficient information about the young woman for my Canadian grandmother to write to her in reply. That correspondence has since been lost. Although my Aunt Shirley, my father's younger sister, recalled its receipt, she remembered very little of the content beyond the young woman's surname, Smith. Of course, that could have been no more than a coincidence. With the trail now cold, the mystery will remain unsolved.

The second disclosure was that, at some point in 1945, my mother and grandparents received a 'welfare' visit from a Canadian official. Though it also could be no more than a coincidence, my father spent a period in hospital in Colchester in the middle of that year, having been transferred there from Germany to recuperate from the fractured leg he suffered on VE Day. Information about that 'welfare' visit led me to wonder whether it had been made at his instigation or through more formal channels as a routine follow-up to my grandfather's earlier complaint, but that also will never be known.

Yet other information, passed on by my Aunt Shirley, suggests that attempts to contact my father could also have been made by my mother or, more probably, one of her sisters acting on her behalf. She recalled that her mother, my paternal grandmother, had received (or perhaps intercepted) a letter from England some time after the war. The correspondence, which may have concerned child support, was not disclosed to my father. Apparently, my grandmother's reply, which pointed out that her son was settling down to life back in Canada, was phrased in such a way as to discourage further communication.

Another strand of evidence, passed on by my adoptive father, who had no reason whatsoever to mislead or misinform, suggests that around the time of the 'welfare' visit the possibility of placing me for adoption was mooted. Fortunately, I was saved from that fate. That was because my grandparents decided against it – my grandmother, because she could not bear to see me go, and my grandfather, because he viewed, or was persuaded to look upon, my arrival in the family as a substitute for the son and heir he and his wife had failed to produce.

While my grandmother's stance was protective, my grandfather's interest was expressed in other ways. In early childhood, I spent many hours in his company, and have happy memories of rides in the front tray of the tradesman's bicycle he then used for travel between his home and the yard alongside Reach Road where he kept some livestock and his farm implements, in horse-drawn tumbrel carts, or seated on the toolbox of his Model N Standard Fordson tractor while he was engaged on fieldwork tasks. Later, when he encouraged me to walk in front of him behind a horse-drawn plough showing me how to set a sightline for a first, straight furrow, or when he demonstrated such other tasks as setting the corner of a stack, mucking out a pigsty or driving a tractor, he was undoubtedly trying to gauge or foster my interest in farm work.

But any hopes he might have nurtured that I would follow in his footsteps were in vain. A final gesture was made on the eve of my departure for university in 1963. It was a last throw of the dice that, for him, fell unfavourably. His alternative was a proposal that I should work alongside him in return for the immediate transfer of ownership of the 5-acre field he had first harvested after his father's death in 1917, plus a sow and her litter, with the prospect of taking over from him when he retired. Though I have never regretted my decision to decline that offer, it has nostalgic associations. After my grandfather's death in 1980, I plucked an ear of wheat grown on that field. It was from his last (ungathered) harvest. Three decades later, it remains in my possession, preserved in a glass jar in my study, an ever-present reminder of what could have been.

A final strand concerns my mother's health. Though there is no doubt about her mental and physical state at the reunion with my adoptive father in March 1946, the assertion that the onset of this condition coincided with my conception and birth did not appear to be reflected in other sources. Although my mother did her utmost to ensure that no paper trail, including my original birth certificate and legal adoption papers, was left behind (she did not anticipate that such information could be obtained through different channels), she was less careful in other ways. The latter included the stock of family photographs. They were less carefully 'edited'. When reviewed after my adoptive father's demise, they were found to contain snaps taken during the first six months or so of my life, one clearly annotated September 1944, in which there are no signs of the physical and mental symptoms she was found to be suffering in 1946.

Nevertheless, there can be no denying that between my conception and birth and my adoptive father's homecoming from Burma, she had been under a great deal of stress from the unplanned pregnancy; coping with her parents' reaction (which, particularly in her father's case, is quite unlikely to have been at all sympathetic); bearing a child out of wedlock; and all the disapproval then associated with unmarried motherhood. There was also the emotional turmoil surrounding the need to consider the option of placing her child for adoption; and, possibly above all, the prospect of meeting her erstwhile boyfriend with a baby son in tow. It could not have been easy for her, and it is not difficult to comprehend how, over time, those experiences must have exerted a toll on her health.

Making sense of those different strands of potential evidence without other sources of corroboration was a formidable challenge. Eventually, I decided to share my findings and suspicions with my mother's youngest sister, the sole surviving 'eye witness'. It was an awkward telephone call in which she was reluctant to engage, not least because it was to test to breaking point my aunt's loyalty to her late sister in obliging her to disclose a longstanding family conspiracy. The outcome was an admission that the rape 'story' was untrue, that it was a fabrication, most probably motivated by a desire to facilitate the reconciliation between my mother and adoptive father on his return from Burma. It proved to be a most effective subterfuge. Throughout the remainder of his life, my adoptive father appears never to have once questioned the veracity of what he had been told.

After putting down the phone, I felt guilty about having subjected my aunt to such a stern interrogation. But it is quite doubtful that the truth about my origins would have been divulged in any other way. So what was that truth, insofar as it can be discerned through the mists of time and deception? In essence, it reveals a much more prosaic story.

It is the story of a headstrong young woman, caught up in the fearful, uncertain, 'live-for-the-moment', social climate of wartime Britain, who was less faithful to any promises made, or assurances given, to a boyfriend before he was posted overseas than – or so it appears – he was to her. However, there was no formal commitment and, as time passed, little or no communication between them. In their absence, she formed a friendship with a member of the overseas services, with whom she shared a passion for dancing. Their relationship blossomed and the inevitable happened. But, by the time her pregnancy was confirmed, that soldier had moved to another, more distant posting. There were, of course, no witnesses to the 'seminal event', but the indication that the relationship might have continued thereafter does not suggest it was non-consensual, let alone violent – although it is quite plausible that what may have been consensual at the time became 'non-consensual' once its consequences were known.

Within a year of my birth, the war in Europe came to an end. The Canadian official's 'welfare' visit to my mother's family home was made around that time. As he was informed that no help was needed, that refusal could be taken to indicate that my mother had decided to set a new course for her life. It is possible, but by no means certain, that the welfare visit had coincided with thoughts of adoption. Whatever had passed between them, it seems that neither my mother nor my father was prepared to commit to a longer-term relationship.

In any event, developments took a different course. With the support of my grandparents, it was decided to keep me within the family fold. A few months later, war in the Far East also ended. Forced to confront her former boyfriend on his homecoming, that additional source of stress, on top of the cumulative impact of others with which she had been obliged to cope, had a catastrophic effect on my mother's psychological reserves, resulting in a nervous breakdown. The 'rape' report was intended to facilitate their reconciliation. Its cost was a whole life sentence served for that deceit.

Given the narrow, parochial and family-focussed horizons within which my mother spent most, if not all, of her post-war life, I imagine her thoughts and actions were governed much more by her subterfuge than any consideration of the possible effects of the deliberate concealment of information about my paternity. But the cover-up, conducted with the full knowledge and complicity of other members of the Smith family, did have other consequences. For instance, how had my adoptive father's (uncorrected) perception of me as a child conceived as a result of the alleged rape shaped the nature and course of our relationship during my childhood and adolescence? More tellingly, perhaps, those consequences also included a golden wedding anniversary celebration in 1996, arranged and attended by my mother's sisters and their families, to which neither my sister Maggie, the child from my mother and adoptive father's marriage, nor I received invitations. In fact, that event came to our notice much later, and then only by chance. (It was perhaps one of the 'damned secrets' that so discomforted my adoptive father.) Presumably, we were not invited because the occasion was likely to have raised issues and questions my mother was still intent to avoid.

I have since had to come to terms with the fact that for most of my life, a very large family circle – and almost certainly others beyond that circle – knew much more about my origins than I did. In the light of what I know now, I very much doubt that any questions that might have been asked earlier would have received truthful answers. Given the history and nature of the cover-up, I believe it most likely that my mother would have stuck to the storyline. She had painted herself into a corner and otherwise would have been compelled to face up to an extremely disquieting dilemma. To tell me the truth about the nature of her relationship with my biological father would have entailed an admission that her later long and generally contented marriage to my adoptive father had been founded on a falsehood. In those circumstances, it seems unlikely she would have altered her story while he was alive. As it was, she predeceased him.

From time to time during my enquiries, the negative sentiment of 'This Be The Verse', Philip Larkin's poem about parental influence, sprung to mind. Its evocation of a spectre of blame was most intensely experienced in the anger and outrage I felt after my mother's death, when Max Clements' identity as my biological father was first disclosed. But those raw emotions have since been replaced by a more sympathetic perspective, time having exercised its healing qualities. Issues surrounding my conception and the subsequent cover-up are now thought to merit regret rather than blame. I shall always regret that my mother chose not to inform me about my paternity, though her reasons for doing so are understandable, and I rue that I never mentioned my suspicions to her. I can see that her actions were not only prompted by guilt, shame and self-preservation, but also, perhaps misguidedly (for that is how it appears to me), to 'protect' me from the truth about my origins.

The context in which those fateful decisions were made is also important. The emotional shadowland of the war, including the insecurity of those who hoped and prayed for the safe return of boyfriends or husbands, is well documented. In those circumstances, it is not too surprising that some British women, both single and married, not all of whom were 'good time girls', sought solace in the friendship and companionship of allied forces. Nor is it surprising that some of those relationships resulted in marriages, although far from satisfactory for some of those war brides. Elsewhere, women caught up in the war encountered much more extreme fates. Many, like the German women who became campaign wives to their Russian invaders, were driven into that role for self-protection or to ensure a supply of food for their children. Others, like the women who were enslaved in brothels to 'service' Japanese troops, had no choice.

Identity

Because it will forever remain behind closed doors, the essence of my biological parents' relationship will always be a matter of conjecture. Nevertheless, even in the event of its proposal, I think it unlikely that my mother would ever have consented to a marriage that would have removed her from her roots, or that she would have made a successful transition to life as a war bride. She was a Smith, generations of whom had lived their entire lives in the same village. She was too firmly set in that mould for such adventure. And so events, which had consequences for all concerned, took a different course.

I have found myself wondering about the extent to which the circumstances into which I was born and my childhood experience have influenced my personality, outlook on life and sense of identity. If truth be told, those who know me at all well would probably agree that I have a generally introverted, introspective disposition and a low sociability 'quotient' (socialising and small talk have never been my forte). They are 'Aspergeresque' traits, reflected in a preference

151

for individual rather than group activities, and uneasiness generally manifest in social settings, at which I have always preferred to keep my own counsel or remain on the sidelines. (Indeed, breaking out of that 'comfort zone' to share this story is one of the hardest decisions I have ever had to make.) This is not the place in which to attempt to resolve the nature/nurture debate, but I would be inclined to conclude that nurture, the pattern of my upbringing, in particular the shallow, emotionally cool and distanced nature of family inter-personal relationships, certainly played its part in shaping my adult personality and behaviour.

Whether or not my mother acted more on impulse than measured reflection, or more out of self-interest than altruistic concern for my welfare, her actions resulted in a childhood and the greater part of my adult life spent in ignorance about my paternal ancestry. That ignorance precluded any contact with my Canadian father or his family while my mother remained alive and insistent that the veil of secrecy should not be lifted. The significance of such deprivation did not strike me immediately. The initial reaction was to view the past as a closed book. Only later did an alternative perspective suggest itself.

It was triggered by two fresh insights. One was the observation of the American clinical psychologist, Mary Pipher, that: '... history is inextricably linked to identity. If you don't know your history, if you don't know your family, who are you?' The other insight sprang from a telephone call with my granddaughter, Beth. She was working on a school project on the Pilgrim Fathers and the Puritan settlement of North America. She wanted to know more about James Babcock, her direct ancestor, going back thirteen generations, who had crossed the Atlantic a decade or so after the voyage of the *Mayflower*. I was delighted to share the story and sent her a photo-graph of the Babcock burial ground in Westerly, Rhode Island, where his bones were laid to rest. In doing so, it made me realise that, at the tender age of nine years, Beth had established a potentially life-long anchoring point with our North American heritage which had eluded me until past retirement age.

The significance of the link between history and identity has been more formally recognised in social science. Scholars from different disciplines – anthropology, psychology, sociology – are broadly agreed that our identity, our sense of self, comprises a complex mix of different determinants. Some originate in the family and kinship network into which we are born and in which we are raised. Others emanate from the more encompassing social settings in which our lives are lived. All embody contemporary attitudes, values and beliefs and more deeply-rooted traditions and cultural determinants passed on from one generation to the next. Clearly, identity – who we are and how others perceive and respond to us – is more than a simple labelling, more than a name registered on an electoral roll or recorded in a passport. It is more complex than Shakespeare's Juliet appears to have had in mind in her protestation 'What's in a name?' Against the background of a longstanding family feud, simply changing his name is unlikely to have had much effect in modifying Romeo's identity as a Montague.

My paternal ancestry was unearthed quite late in the day, when I was in my sixties and already set in my ways. It was certainly too late to have any significant influence on my personality or outlook on life. Yet what I learned about that family background was not entirely without value, especially for the light it seemed to shed, albeit retrospectively, on my responses to some of the events that might be said to have shaped my destiny.

For example, in both halves of my family tree, the predominant occupational pattern over generations is of lives and (insofar as there was freedom to choose) preferences that were firmly rooted in rural soil and so commitment to a lifestyle which, in George Mackay Brown's words, was informed by 'earth wisdom' and regulated by 'the uncertain wheel of agriculture'. Although throughout my ancestors' lifetimes national economies were developing and diversifying, generating new jobs and opportunities, those ancestors mostly seem to have found such options unattractive. There is little evidence of movement from the countryside to towns or cities, or from farming and associated rural activities into the rapidly

153

expanding worlds of industry, commerce or the professions. Their preferred lifestyle, governed by the rhythm of the seasons rather than the higher tempo and repetitive nature of most tasks performed in factories, shops and offices, is one with which I can strongly empathise. It has been reflected in my own occupational preferences in which the seasonal beat of agriculture could be said to have been substituted by the annual cycle of the academic year or the often slower tempo of research projects or programmes that may take several years from inception to production of final reports and associated publications.

Though my choice of career may reflect both maternal and paternal influences, its conduct, which entailed some significant risk-taking and life-course changing moves, could with the benefit of hindsight be viewed as reflecting a more one-sided paternal influence. Discoveries about my paternal ancestors have yielded insights into the previously inexplicable sense of semi-detachment, of difference or 'outsiderness' I experienced as a child and into adulthood. In a line of direct descent, I was the very first Smith in at least seven generations, most probably many more, to resist the gravitational pull of kinship and locality. Whereas my maternal great grand-parents, grandparents and my mother and her sisters, and also family members of my own generation have either spent their lives in Burwell or settled within a bicycle ride or short car journey from the village, my life has followed a more itinerant and, I believe, more adventurous course. It suggests to me that, if there is a 'gene' for adventure, in the sense of preparedness to confront the unknown, to countenance and cope with change, it is markedly less evident in the Smith family's make-up than that of my paternal forebears.

With characteristic perceptiveness, Jorge Luis Borges once wrote: 'Any life, no matter how long and complex it may be, is made up of a single moment – the moment in which a man finds out once and for all who he is.' For me, that moment of self-knowledge, of awareness of the fundamental relationship between history and identity, was linked to the unearthing of my Canadian roots.

Certainly, if on some future date I have the opportunity to repeat the flight over Lake Erie I first made in 1983, when I had those first, distant glimpses of southwestern Ontario and the land on which my paternal forebears settled, that landscape would be viewed in an entirely different light. I would be looking down on much more than a tract of Canada's physical geography. I would be viewing a social and cultural landscape in which I found not only ancestral roots but also, much more importantly, the love of my father's family and unconditional acceptance into their midst.

If somehow the sharing of this account of my journey to, and travel within, that family hinterland paves the way for other war children to achieve similar outcomes, there could be no greater reward. But for that to become a reality, the plight of Canada's war children needs to be viewed in an entirely new light. It should be regarded as a matter of basic human rights, reflecting their genetic inheritance, their 'blood ties', rather than a matter of 'nationality' or 'citizenship', the legal parameters within which, to date, their searching for paternal roots has been sidelined and judged.

Afterword: The Case for Recognition and Reconciliation

The family reunion at the Corunna branch of the Royal Canadian Legion in May 2010 marked an end to the journey on which I had embarked five years earlier. At journey's end, I had achieved so much more than I ever thought possible at its outset. I had traced my late father's immediate family and wider kinship network. Their humanity and decency had ensured I received the warmest imaginable welcome into their midst. Moreover, through confirmation of my Anglo-Canadian identity, links had been forged with generations of paternal ancestors who had participated in, or whose lives had been touched by, many of the events that had shaped the development of the North American continent since the seventeenth century.

In personal terms, those outcomes were immensely gratifying and offered closure to my quest. Yet that sense of closure remained incomplete. Despite the good fortune that ensured the most favourable of possible outcomes for my own enquiries, my thoughts continued to turn to the many other war children who had been born in similar circumstances, but whose attempts to trace fathers or paternal families had failed, foundered or met with outright rejection.

My experience may show that, at least in cases in which there are clear leads to follow, it may be possible to circumvent the many legislative and bureaucratic obstacles 'Fortress Canada' has erected to deflect legitimate enquiries concerning paternity. In sharing that experience, I hope it will help to achieve four broader objectives. The first is that it will encourage other war children to commence or renew their own searches. The second is that it will persuade Canadian veterans or their families, who previously have denied paternity or otherwise distanced themselves from such enquiries, to relent and reconsider those decisions. The third is that it will prompt a more searching analysis of this chapter of Canada's history which, to date, seems to have received little if any encouragement, let alone official endorsement. Fourthly, of more overriding concern, it is hoped it will encourage Canadians to examine their national conscience and consider how to implement fairer, more humane and 'inclusive' policy and practice in this sphere. In July 2010, Queen Elizabeth II visited Winnipeg to unveil a cornerstone of the Canadian Museum of Human Rights. On that occasion, the Prime Minister, Stephen Harper, is reported to have observed that his country is the '... steward of a precious legacy of human rights... Canada's conscience has been formed by a profound belief in human rights and this living tradition of freedom... It has made us a good country.' But Canada's longstanding disavowal of any responsibility for its war children could be thought to cast a shadow of doubt over that proud assertion.

Who are those war children? They are Canada's unacknowledged *untermenschen*, the record of whose perception and treatment by the Canadian establishment discloses more than a whiff – more a palpable odour – of negative eugenics and institutional misogyny. Born out of wedlock between 1940 and 1946 from relationships between their mothers and Canadian servicemen, they are thought to number about 30,000, around 22,000 of whom were born in Britain, the remainder in other European states, mainly The Netherlands. Their actual number remains unknown. No interest has ever been shown in collecting and collating a more detailed statistical record, either in Canada or in the countries of their birth.

At the time of writing (2012), the war children are mostly in their late sixties and early seventies, generally living settled lives in retirement, with children and grandchildren of their own. Quite understandably, many have nurtured desires to 'connect' with their fathers. But few have achieved that ambition. Many more have tried and failed, not through lack of effort on their part, but because they were spurned or denied access to the records needed to begin their search. With each passing year, as demonstrated by the rapidly-dwindling attendances of Second World War veterans at Remembrance Day parades, more and more of the war children's fathers have passed away (surviving fathers would now be at least in their late eighties). It would be quite wrong, however, to conclude that their demise has in any way lessened the desire their children still nurture to establish that connection with paternal kith and kin.

Possibly reflecting an enduring official indifference to their existence, an embarrassment that was best kept under wraps, information about Canada's treatment of its war children is sparse. Melynda Jarratt, a leading advocate for war brides' issues and one of the few social historians to have studied this topic, has pointed out in one of her contributions to *Voices of the Left Behind* that no systematic, in-depth research appears to have been undertaken. Indeed, given glimpses into official thinking about the war children that can be gleaned indirectly from different sources, government sponsorship or encouragement of such investigations was perhaps always quite unlikely.

An appreciation of why this is the case begs consideration of several different, if potentially interlocking, strands of evidence. They include the evolution of Canada's law relating to citizenship; the official mindset that appears to have guided the framing of the Canadian Citizenship Act, 1946; the social and political context of that decision-making process; and the feasibility of implementing alternative, more sympathetic approaches which embody principles of natural justice and *jus sanguinis* without undermining the integrity of Canada's law on citizenship, privacy and access to information.

The legal framework

Canada's law on citizenship originated from the 1946 act. Before that legislation came into force on 1 January 1947, Canadians, whether by birth or naturalisation, were formally designated as British subjects with Canadian nationality, with that status conferred by other pre-existing law on nationality, naturalisation and immigration. The lack of a more definitive, statute-based definition of citizenship was a source of growing concern between the two world wars, as Canada became increasingly aware of its developing importance as a world power, especially towards the end of the Second World War. It is widely held that the most important catalyst for change was a visit in the final year of the war that the Cabinet member, Paul Martin (senior), made to war graves in Dieppe, the location of the ill-fated raid in August 1942 that resulted in a significant sacrifice of Canadian lives. Apparently, he was so moved by attributions to the British subject status of the fallen, over and above their Canadian nationality that, with prime ministerial and Cabinet backing, he introduced a bill to Canada's House of Commons in October 1945 which aimed to provide for the first time in his country's history a unifying, legally-based definition of Canadian citizenship. In introducing his bill, he described its aims in the following terms:

> For the national unity of Canada and for the future and greatness of this country it is felt to be of utmost importance that all of us, new Canadians or old, have a consciousness of a common purpose and common interests as Canadians; that all of us are able to say with pride and say with meaning: 'I am a Canadian citizen.'

Undoubtedly, the enactment of Paul Martin's bill into law in 1946 as 'An Act respecting Citizenship, Nationality, Naturalization and Status of Aliens', better known as The Canadian Citizenship Act, 1946, marked a significant landmark in Canada's constitutional history. It provided a common unifying basis for the newly-defined citizenship of Canada's existing population. It also set out parameters for the future admission of others seeking to immigrate and acquire citizenship status through naturalisation. But it was not without flaws and there was a need for amending legislation before its eventual repeal and replacement by new legislation, The Canadian Citizenship Act, 1976. A principal aim of that legislation was to remedy a discriminatory distinction between the entitlement to citizenship of children born outside of Canada to a Canadian father, whose entitlement was assured by the 1946 legislation, and those born in similar circumstances to a Canadian mother, who previously had no such entitlement, so that a parent of either sex now had the right to pass on Canadian citizenship to children born abroad.

But that remedy was also incomplete – in particular because it did not embrace those born between 1 January 1947, when the first act took effect, and 14 February 1977, the day before the second act came into force. That was mainly because of misgivings expressed at the committee stage of the latter legislation about the potentially unknown consequences of retroactive or retrospective application of the new law.

Much later, after the attack on New York's twin towers in September 2001, as part of its War on Terror and perceived need for enhanced homeland security, the United States imposed stricter border controls. Those changes obliged Canadians, who previously were able to enter and leave the United States with few formalities, to apply for or renew passports. That development contributed to the identification of various categories of 'Lost Canadians'. Amongst others, they included some of the war brides who thought they had Canadian citizenship but who discovered, when making passport applications, that it had been inadvertently forfeited. They also included 'military brats', the children of Canadian armed services' personnel born between 1947 and 1977, when their parents were living and serving in other countries.

Bill C-37, An Act to Amend the Citizenship Act, which came into force in May 2009, restored or conferred citizenship for many of those 'Lost Canadians'. But some war children, a select minority who had been born out of wedlock before 1947 but who had accompanied their war bride mothers to Canada after the war and subsequently spent their lives with both parents in Canada; and who hoped that the new legislation would also grant them previously denied Canadian citizenship, were not deemed to merit similarly favourable treatment.

Like their counterparts (the vast majority of the war children who have never lived in Canada, and whose main concern has been to trace fathers rather than to seek Canadian citizenship), those war children were excluded principally on the grounds that they were born out of wedlock before January 1947 and were officially deemed at birth to have acquired their mothers' nationality. So it remains the case that no war child has ever had rights, entitlements or other claims under Canadian law, even if he or she could demonstrate relationship to their veteran father through their parents' later marriage, the inclusion of their father's name on a birth certificate, other evidence of paternity that relatives might have provided or through genetic testing; and even though the recent 'Lost Canadians' legislation has retroactively confirmed the right to citizenship of any child born after 1 January 1947 to a parent of either sex who already had Canadian citizenship. It appears it is now only those who were born out of wedlock before 1947 who are still treated differently.

To shed light on this chapter in Canada's history, it seems there would need to be a review of records stored in the darkest recesses of the country's national archives. It would appear that, while the war children's fate was formally sealed during the year before the Canadian Citizenship Act, 1946 came into effect, there were deeper roots to the attitudes and opinions (if not prejudice) which informed the act itself and all subsequent amendments of Canada's citizenship law.

The plight of the war children is well illustrated by the case of Joseph Taylor. He was born out of wedlock in England in December 1944. His mother was English. His father, Joseph Taylor (senior), was a Canadian serviceman. Before he took part in the D-

Day landings, Joseph Taylor (senior) had sought permission to marry, only to be denied, a decision that reflected what was by then a well-entrenched deterrent policy of discouragement and delay. In the event, Joseph Taylor's parents married in May 1945, between his father's return to England from service elsewhere in Europe and repatriation to Canada in February 1946. Arrangements were then made for his wife and son to join him at his home on Vancouver Island, a journey made on the strength of the assurance given to all war brides that, on arrival, they would be awarded Canadian citizenship. Sadly, the marriage was short-lived. In the absence of any help or support, Mrs Taylor opted to return to England with her son, making that journey, for which she was issued a Canadian passport, in October 1946.

Joseph Taylor spent both his formative and most of his adult years in England. Around 1971, aged twenty-six and married with children of his own, he explored the possibility, as the son of a Second World War Canadian veteran with a history of residence in Canada in his own right, of moving to his father's country of birth. For various reasons, which may not have been made clear to him at the time, his case was handled as a conventional application for immigration for which sponsorship was needed. His efforts to contact his father to secure his sponsorship were unsuccessful and the matter was not taken further. In 1999, after a visit to Canada, Joseph Taylor tried again, only to be advised that any earlier claim to Canadian citizenship he might have had had been forfeited on his twenty-fourth birthday in December 1968. Undeterred, he proceeded with two attempts in 2003 to obtain certification of his Canadian citizenship. Both failed. The first was turned down on grounds that he had lost his entitlement in 1968. The second attempt was rejected on grounds that, since he had been born out of wedlock before the 1946 act came into force, he did not have, and had never had, citizenship status.

Joseph Taylor then sought a judicial review of the latter decision. The case was heard in the Federal Court, Vancouver, in May, 2006. The judgment, delivered at Ottawa in September 2006, was in the applicant's favour. It set aside the citizenship officer's contested decision, declared Joseph Taylor to be a Canadian citizen and directed the minister to issue him with a certificate of Canadian citizenship. However, any sense of triumph Joseph Taylor might have experienced did not last. At the minister's instigation, the case was referred to the Federal Court of Appeal, where it was heard in Vancouver in September 2007. The judgment, delivered at Ottawa two months later, overturned the earlier Federal Court decision. Its effect was to deprive Joseph Taylor of his recently-awarded, much sought-after citizenship, although it was pointed out that the avenue to citizenship through naturalisation could still be open to him.

In the event, he was not obliged to follow that route. In December 2007, Joseph Taylor was granted Canadian citizenship through the Minister of Citizenship and Immigration's exercise of a discretionary power to confer that status in exceptional circumstances. That decision could be construed as a politically astute, face-saving gesture, since at the time the government was also embroiled in an ongoing debate about the legal status of other 'Lost Canadians'. However, its broader effect was to leave unchanged the implication of the Court of Appeal judgment that Joseph Taylor's status under Canadian law (before the discretionary award of citizenship) was no different from that of other war children. It is ironic that his long struggle to assert his claim to Canadian citizenship would not have been met by the more recent 'Lost Canadians' legislation, the 'mopping-up' exercise in which the war children (including the small minority who had spent their lives in Canada), born out of wedlock before January 1947, were still deemed to remain beyond the pale.

Where the strict interpretation and application of law are concerned, jurists, politicians and bureaucrats cannot be said to have acted other than correctly. But other questions remain. They include whether, over the years, the collective actions of Canada's establishment have delivered or denied natural justice to the war children, not all of whom – possibly only a small minority – wish to assert a claim to Canadian citizenship. They also include questions about the significance of the date on which the Canadian Citizenship Act, 1946 took effect, in particular whether it was merely coincidental or, at least in part, a convenient contrivance that helped to shield some of Canada's veterans from having to accept responsibility for the illegitimate children they fathered and left behind.

The official mindset

Though foundations may have been laid beforehand, Melynda Jarratt's research suggests that the key decisions about the war children were taken in the course of a meeting of the Cabinet Committee on Demobilization and Re-establishment on 9 December 1946. A month earlier, shortly after his return from a visit to the United Kingdom, D.C. Abbott, the Minister of National Defence, had sought the views of a Cabinet sub-committee on four potentially problematic issues arising from the stationing of Canadian forces overseas. They concerned dependents remaining overseas, including those who might never elect to travel to Canada; bigamous marriages; unmarried mothers whose children's paternity had been acknowledged by their Canadian servicemen fathers; and those whose children's paternity had not been similarly acknowledged.

The fate of the mothers and children in the latter two categories was sealed at that meeting, the sub-committee having decided to 'disown' responsibility for their plight, striking them off from further consideration. That decision was ratified at the Cabinet Committee meeting on 9 December when, on the eve of his retirement, a short report by D.C. Abbott on 'Problems Related to Wives and Dependents Residing Overseas', which included the recommendation that: 'No provision is made for financial aid to mothers of illegitimate children or for the care and maintenance of such children', was formally endorsed. The Canadian Government's official disavowal of responsibility for the war children was finally confirmed twenty-four days later, when the Canadian Citizenship Act, 1946 came into force.

Other sources suggest those measures had deeper roots. For example, in *Saints, Sinners, and Soldiers*, a well-documented history of Canada's home front during the Second World War, Jeffrey E. Keshen devotes his final chapter to the preparations made for the repatriation and re-establishment of the country's veterans. He notes that such planning commenced within months of Canada's entry into the war, mainly in response to concerns voiced by First World War veterans about the need to avoid shortcomings such as those they had experienced in the arrangements made for their return after 1918 (although Canada was far from alone in its failure to ensure adequate post-war provision for jobs, homes and other much needed support).

From Keshen's account, the Canadian Government's response commenced as early as December 1939, with the creation of a Cabinet Committee on Demobilization and Re-establishment under the direction of Ian Mackenzie, Minister of Pensions and National Health and a former vice-president of the Great War Veterans' Association. He had already lobbied the prime minister, Mackenzie King, about the need for early action. In turn, the Cabinet Committee established an advisory sub-committee. Two of the most influential sub-committee members were said to be Robert England, its executive secretary and former director of the Royal Canadian Legion's educational service, and Walter S. Woods, the Associate Deputy Minister of Pensions and National Health and former chair of the War Veterans' Allowance Board. Both had been wounded while serving in the First World War. After the war, both had devoted their time to veterans' organisations and affairs.

As Keshen records, from their establishment in late 1939 to the creation of the Department of Veterans Affairs in March 1944, those committees worked jointly to lay foundations for what was to become the post-war Veterans Charter. Ever mindful that their task could influence the morale of forces in the field, a series of measures were taken from 1941 onward to ensure that discharged personnel would be entitled to not only quite generous tax-exempt honourable discharge gratuities, but also such other benefits as assistance with education, vocational training or employment; tax-exempt funding to help them with the cost of setting up a home or business; or grants or subsidised loans to those who opted for self-employment in commercial fishing or farming.

Hand in hand with those measures, other departments, including those of Defence, External Affairs, and Mines and Resources (which was then responsible for immigration), were also involved in arrangements for the resettlement of armed forces personnel and their dependents, for whom a major transportation exercise was needed, beginning as early as 1941, but which developed into a much more substantial operation in the immediate post-war years. As noted in a *History of the Directorate of Repatriation of Servicemen's Dependents*, prepared in 1947 by Col G. Ellis, Director of Repatriation, Department of Defence, passages to Canada were arranged for not only the country's troops but also, between August 1944 and January 1947, 41,351 war brides and their 19,737 children. The latter were additional to 1,109 wives and 578 children who travelled to Canada before August 1944, and more who were to follow after January 1947.

Other steps were taken to prepare troops for their homecoming and to alert their families and communities about changes they might see in the personalities and outlook of those who were returning home. In those respects, Keshen describes various initiatives to promote the Veterans Charter and enhance service personnel's appreciation of what was on offer, including the financial aspects and the resettlement options and opportunities that would be available to them. Other measures aimed to inform them about ways in which life on the home front might have changed during their absence, in particular how wartime absorption into the labour market might have modified women's perception of their role in society. At the same time, parents, wives, sisters and girlfriends were forewarned about the war-wrought 'rough edges' their sons, husbands, brothers or boyfriends could exhibit. Reflecting specific concerns over the availability of jobs for the returning forces, and the likely effect on the marital relationships of men who were expecting their womenfolk to fulfil no more than conventional pre-war, homemaker roles, hints that women should consider stepping aside from their paid employment outside the home were not uncommon features of that groundwork publicity.

There are reasons to suspect that Canada's rejection of its war children also dates from the early years of the war. Soon after the first of its armed forces were drafted to Britain in late 1939, alarms were raised about the number of servicemen who were requesting permission to marry. The official response was one of deterrence and discouragement, expressed in delays in dealing with such requests and the imposition of a stipulation that they would not be granted unless servicemen could demonstrate that they had accumulated a specified level of savings.

Those alarm bells rang not only in the Department of Defence but also in the Immigration Branch of the Department of Mines and Resources. As early as January 1942, Col N.O. Lawson, Director of Supplies and Transport, Department of National Defence (Army) contacted F.C. Blair, Director of the Immigration Branch in the Department of Mines and Resources for general guidance on issues relating to the repatriation to Canada of dependents of the country's armed forces stationed overseas. In addition to other more general matters, Mr Blair's reply included the following cautionary observation:

> Towards the close and after the last war, our Department handled the repatriation of approximately 50,000 soldiers' dependents… In numerous cases questions of settlement arose as presumably they will this time. We also had to deal with a certain undesirable element as, for example, we found dependents who were physically, mentally and morally unfit. Under the Canadian Immigration Act and regulations, marriage to a soldier does not *ipso facto* place the wife in the position of a non-immigrant; she is still subject to immigration inspection and certain restrictions relating to health and character.

That was not the only reference to the perceived undesirable element. F.C. Blair was to reiterate his views, both in committee and in other written communications. For example, a telegram sent to C.V. Massey, High Commissioner for Canada in Great Britain, in February 1942 included references to prospective immigrants belonging to 'prohibited classes', in that instance those thought likely to become a burden on Canada's public finances, who were to be excluded from repatriation arrangements. Around the same time, he wrote a letter to Lester B. Pearson, a future prime minister, diplomat of international renown and Nobel Laureate, who was then serving in the Department of External Affairs under Louis St Laurent, Mackenzie King's successor as prime minister in 1948, in which the views of the Immigration Branch were set out a little more fully:

> In answer to Mr. Massey's (b) I may say that what we told our London office was that repatriation would not extend to immigrants belonging to prohibited classes. The wives and children who have not been resident in Canada must enter as immigrants. If history repeats itself we will find some women and children feeble-minded, insane or otherwise mentally defective who thereby come in the excluded classes. We found this class amongst those repatriated after the last war. We wanted to make clear to our London office that repatriation was not to be given to persons who may be rejected on such grounds.

Taken at face value, there is nothing overtly objectionable about the stance taken by the Immigration Branch in its role as Canada's official gatekeeper; every nation has an indisputable right to exercise control over who is or is not granted admission to its territory. In Canada's case, the precedent was set with the establishment of a quarantine station on Grosse Ile in 1832, thirty-five years before dominion status was granted by the British North America Act, 1867. Dominion status enabled the federal government to pass and develop its own laws. One of the earliest pieces of legislation was the

Immigration Act, 1869. It was the forerunner of seven later Immigration Acts, which were themselves subject to numerous intervening pieces of amending legislation. In conjunction with other legislation dealing with nationality and citizenship issues, a body of law of such Byzantine complexity was created that it is arguable that even the most recent amendment of the law relating to citizenship, dealing with the 'Lost Canadians', has failed to remove all of its rough edges.

One recurring theme within that body of law has been its concern with statutorily defined 'proscribed', 'excluded' or 'prohibited' classes of prospective immigrants, the 'undesirable element' who were targeted in F.C. Blair's wartime communications. Reflecting the Grosse Ile precedent, the earliest concerns related to health issues. Prevention of communicable disease was the primary aim of the 1869 legislation, and has remained so. However, over time, the list of those considered to be undesirable was expanded to include (to repeat some of the now unacceptable pejorative labelling then in common use) such other categories as the feeble-minded, the mentally defective, the insane, former mental asylum patients, other disabled, epileptics, convicted criminals, persons who had been charged with but not convicted of a serious offence, homosexuals, prostitutes, paupers, and yet others who at different times were discriminated against on grounds of race or nationality. In brief, to revert to F.C. Blair's shorter description, the 'physically, mentally and morally unfit'.

This is not to challenge Canada's undoubted sovereign right to exercise choice over who is admitted to its realm, nor is it intended in any way to pillory or malign the character of the wartime Director of the Immigration Branch of the Department of Mines and Resources. Since his views appear to have passed without challenge – moreover, to have reflected official government policy – it would seem that they were representative of a widely-shared mindset in his department, if not more generally within the ranks of the Canadian establishment. Rather, the purpose in drawing attention to that mindset is to highlight for contemporary consideration the possibility that, whether inadvertently or by design, at some point toward the end of the Second World War, if not earlier, the unmarried mothers of Canada's war children, the disowned *untermenschen*, were unjustifiably categorised alongside all other undesirable persons and that, in consequence, they were cast as the unwitting scapegoats of a post-war moral crisis in Canada. Not content with its implicit vilification of those mothers while exonerating the fathers, the Canadian Government, in its infinite wisdom, saw fit to visit the mothers' 'sins' on the children through the creation and maintenance of a series of legislative and bureaucratic barriers, still in place in 2012, designed to shelter their fathers and paternal kith and kin.

The social and political context

That Canada ended the war in a state of moral crisis is beyond doubt. Jeffrey E. Keshen's carefully documented analysis chronicles the many and various parameters within which that crisis found expression. Noting 'Apprehensive, and sometimes panicked reactions to wartime immorality and social instability', his history of Canada's home front records and reports markedly increased trends of illegitimacy, abortions, marital infidelity, venereal disease, delinquency, quickie marriages, and divorce, all of which were offensive to the essentially conservative ethos of a society keen to re-establish the pre-war social and moral *status quo*.

But the world had moved on. The veterans, whose wartime experiences had resulted in changes in behaviour, outlook and values, returned home to a society which also differed from the one from which they had sailed only a few years earlier. Understandably, there was concern on the part of Canada's leadership about the potentially destabilising effect of those social changes. But, in a classic demonstration of the social mechanisms of stereotyping and prejudice, an evident reluctance to assign blame internally seems to have resulted in its projection onto 'outsiders', the unmarried mothers of its forces' war children.

Keshen's conclusion is that many post-war political and social policy initiatives, including those dealing with veterans' concerns, were: '... designed to achieve more effective control over behaviour, and thus had a conservative, perhaps even a reactionary, quality.' Less explicit, but no less significant, was a compact that appears to have been made with those veterans in pursuit of the government's aim to achieve greater social stability, that they would be shielded from the consequences of any past 'indiscretions'. How else should the Department of Veterans Affairs' reluctance to deal more effectively than it is said to have done with post-war enquiries about child support be construed? Keshen cites an example of prevailing advice from a post-war columnist: 'If you have a secret that would make the one who loves you unhappy to know, bury it in your soul... The war ended one phase of your life. You are now starting another.'

The tacit endorsement this advice to bury the past seems to have received in official circles could also reflect an even earlier, publicly unspoken compact between former members of Canada's armed forces who survived the First World War, officers and other ranks alike, who never disclosed their dalliances with *les dames et demoiselles d'Armentières* and in other 'behind the lines' locations like Amiens, in which sexual services were readily available in *maisons tolérées* and other similar, if less salubrious, establishments. Whether, like Dennis Wheatley, members of Canada's First World War officer class themselves took advantage of those 'blue lamp' services for those in higher ranks or whether, like Robert Graves, they remained chaste, they must have been aware of either fellow officers' use of such facilities or other ranks' resort to the 'red light' premises that sprang up in abundance to meet their needs. They must also have been aware of the inevitable spread of venereal disease, about which very little may have been said on the soldiers' return home. Perhaps the former First World War officers, who helped to determine the war children's fate, looking back on their own wartime experience in Europe, were persuaded to view most if not all of the mothers of those children as promiscuous, without any supporting evidence for such a misogynistic opinion.

In the domestic context, the Canadian Citizenship Act, 1946 can be viewed as a subtext to the Veterans Charter. The exclusion of children born out of wedlock before 1947 to mothers who did not have Canadian nationality effectively excused (some might say conveniently contrived to excuse) the veterans who had fathered those illegitimate children from any legal or financial responsibility. Thus, compared to later generations, the veterans received unparalleled protection. As in Max Clements' case, that protection allowed the veterans to move on, to marry and raise families in Canada.

In fairness, the war children's mothers also moved on during the post-war years. In some cases, including my own, they married men who were prepared to take on the Canadians' children, raising them as part of their families. In all too many cases, though, those children were raised by lone parents; by grandparents (often under the guise of being their mother's sibling) or other relatives; placed for adoption; or abandoned in residential childcare institutions.

For several decades after the war, the war children's mothers seemed prepared to keep their secrets, to let matters lie. It was only later, after the children themselves started to discover the truth, that enquiries began and efforts were made to trace their fathers. But · those efforts, associated with a burgeoning sense of injustice, were frequently frustrated by official indifference, obfuscation and obstruction.

That stonewalling response from Canadian officialdom might have been anticipated from the debate preceding the Canadian Citizenship Act, 1976, which was characterised by concern about unknown consequences of retroactive application of the proposed new law. One example – quoted in the Federal Court of Appeal judgment in Joseph Taylor's case – is the evidence in February 1976 of L. Levy, Director of Legal Services, Department of the Secretary of State:

Now we are proposing to create a complete equality in there which would mean that children will derive their citizenship from either parent whether born in wedlock or not. If we were to go back to provide a sort of retroactive catchall there, the government and the country would be in the position of having to accept citizens of all sorts of – perhaps this might sound a little farfetched but if you want to go back to say the Korean war or Canadian Forces policing expeditions in the Middle East or in Cyprus and so on, and assuming that some of the members of the forces may have been active, and more active than others and they had children, they would have the right to have them declared Canadians and bring them into the country. That is just one thing. You do not know what you would be sweeping up; they might be people that if they were to apply for immigration, the Immigration Department would not want to let them in.

Two aspects of that evidence are worth noting. The first is that there is no reference to the illegitimate offspring of Second World War veterans; they had already been consigned to history's dustbin. The second is that the observation: 'You do not know what (N.B. not who) you would be sweeping up' suggests that the ghostly prejudices of F.C. Blair and his contemporaries were still lurking in Ottawa's corridors of power in the mid-1970s.

The airbrushing of the war children did not end there. For example, if the Royal Canadian Legion has or has ever had a formally-adopted policy position on the status of Second World War veterans' illegitimate war children, it does not appear ever to have been publicly aired. An article published in the May/June 2007 issue of the *Legion Magazine* included a brief passing reference to 'war babies', but said no more about them. Its main focus was on two other groups, both reflecting the Legion's then ongoing involvement in the debate on 'Lost Canadians'. Following endorsement of their cause at the Legion's annual convention in 2006, one group was the war brides whose citizenship status was, for various reasons, in doubt. The other group embraced the children of military personnel who had been born between 1947 and 1977 during a parent's overseas posting. However, the Legion's subsequent written and oral evidence to the Parliamentary Standing Committee on Citizenship and Immigration, to which its presentations on 'Lost Canadians' were given, did not include any mention of the war children born before 1947. They remained in limbo.

It is not without relevance that, in the course of its sittings between 2005 and 2008, the Parliamentary Standing Committee on Citizenship and Immigration heard other undoubtedly well-intentioned evidence in which war children were described as 'Canadian bastards'. While that description might be excused on the grounds that its use was intended deliberately to illustrate the negative tone of widely-prevailing attitudes, it beggars belief that the committee allowed it to enter the record of their proceedings without so much as a comment on the appropriateness of such terminology. Equally surprising is the Chair of the Standing Committee's admission, after hearing evidence at its meeting in Fredericton, New Brunswick in April 2005: 'I find it incredibly disturbing that the department – and I've been on this committee a long time – never came forward. I seem to be finding out all kinds of stuff. I never even thought about the illegitimate children, supposedly, of servicemen and that we had totally washed our hands of this.' That admission seems not to have been followed up in the Standing Committee members' later deliberations on 'Lost Canadians'. Should that be taken to imply that its members also have yet to be convinced that the war children have a justifiable cause?

Although Col G. Ellis, the Department of Defence's Director of Repatriation did not refer explicitly to the war children in the report he compiled in 1947 on the work of his directorate, it is beyond belief that he was unaware of their existence. The report was prepared shortly after his return from a visit to Britain, during which – given his official position – he must almost certainly have received detailed military and diplomatic briefings. If so, the conclusion of his report on repatriation arrangements may make strange reading:

In conclusion it should be observed that this was the first time any government had provided a home-to-home service, with amenities, for dependents of their servicemen. It should be considered a selected immigration of very fine stock, which mainly came from the smaller centres of the British Isles to their new homes in Canada. They were in the main above average and the children were far above average in health and mentality.

Though the basis of those 'selected' is clear – they were war brides or fiancées committed to marry within three months of arrival in Canada and their children – with whom were their lauded attributes compared if not the unmarried mothers and their children? What evidence was available to Col Ellis other than military or diplomatic hearsay?

Throughout and immediately after the war, the Historical Section of the London-based Canadian Military Headquarters (CMHQ) was under the leadership and direction of Col Charles Perry Stacey, an eminent historian and later the author of two of the three volumes which comprised the *Official History of the Canadian Army in the Second World War*. The Historical Section prepared an extensive series of detailed reports on all aspects of operational matters and the military and civil circumstances of the Canadian forces while they were stationed in Britain. The latter reports did not pull any punches, covering subjects that were as widely ranging as the poor quality of their accommodation, drunken and riotous episodes in town centres, criminal offences ranging from minor theft to murder, and bigamous marriages.

In contrast, no Historical Section report has been located which refers to the results of informal enquiries, let alone more formally-conducted surveys, which addressed the geographical location, social status and character of the mothers who gave birth to the Canadians' illegitimate war children, or the nature of those mothers' relationships with the servicemen involved. Much has been written (both salacious and more balanced) about wartime moral laxity, prostitution and the exploits of the 'good time girls'. However, many if not most of the women who actually gave birth to children were more probably in what they were persuaded to believe were more stable and loving relationships, more 'innocent' and, hence, less likely to rely on contraception, resort to abortions or pass their infants for adoption.

It might also be considered inconceivable that Col Stacey and his staff were unaware of the existence of those women and their children, but there is no reference to them in the *Official History* (which, incidentally, also lauds the war brides as 'most excellent citizens'). Stacey's later work, *The Half-Million: The Canadians in Britain 1939–1946* (co-authored with Barbara Wilson and published in 1987), does refer to the war children, but only briefly. Their more restricted focus was on around 400 cases in which British civil court maintenance orders were made and an even smaller number of cases in which either Canadian soldiers made voluntary assignments in favour of their illegitimate offspring or the Dependents' Allowance Board made awards to children born out of wedlock. Consequently, their work fails to give an accurate impression of the true scale of the Canadian armed forces' legacy of illegitimate children.

So it would seem that generally Canada's historians have been strongly inclined to ignore this aspect of their country's wartime history. It is possible that such civilian 'intelligence' was gathered covertly, but has since remained classified or otherwise undisclosed. Should that prove to be the case, if there is a factual basis for the aspersions cast by Col Ellis, Col Stacey and their contemporaries in Canada's military and political establishment, is it not time for such evidence to be made public?

If more detailed investigations are undertaken to shed light on this corner of Canadian history, there is at least one other issue that merits greater illumination. It concerns the foundations for the belief expressed by F.C. Blair that special measures were needed to guard against an influx of the 'undesirable element' among the dependents who were expected to accompany or follow in the wake of the country's repatriated armed service personnel. Seemingly, it was a belief that was quite widely shared or 'swallowed' by his First World War officer class contemporaries, who occupied some of the most senior positions in government and the civil service in 1939 and following years. If files relating to the 50,000 cases of service-men's dependents who sought admission to Canada after the First World War, from which F.C. Blair and others derived their clearly influential opinion, are still available, a review could be quite enlightening. It should reveal whether the warnings they felt obliged to give had a firm foundation, and were not simply an exercise in Blimpish scaremongering that ultimately contributed to both the scapegoating of many war children's mothers and the measures taken to frustrate their children's attempts to contact their fathers or paternal relatives.

Reconciliation

The Federal Court of Appeal Judgment in Joseph Taylor's case can be viewed as a once-and-for-all attempt on the part of the judiciary to put war children's claims to Canadian citizenship on the back-burner of history. Within the context of Canada's citizenship law, on two grounds, it was probably correct to do so. First, it reaffirmed the unchallengeable authority of the definition of citizenship in the Canadian Citizenship Act, 1946 and later citizenship legislation. Secondly, if only at the time, it established the unacceptability of claims like those which Joseph Taylor made regarding alleged breach of his rights under Canada's Bill of Rights and the Canadian Charter of Human Rights because of the inappropriateness of their retro-active or retrospective application. Hence Décary J.A.'s concluding observations:

> It seems to me it would be unfair to the parliament and to the government of that day to judge moral values of a distant past in the light of today's values. It could also be an unbearable burden on today's government to demonstrate today that the measures taken then were then justified in a free and demo-cratic society.... All this is to suggest that courts may not be the best instruments for rewriting history.

However, the implication of that judgment – that the past should not be re-visited – should not be allowed to pass unchallenged. Through no fault of their own, the war children have been the innocent victims of an official mindset, coloured by negative eugenics and misogynistic beliefs and opinion. It is simply not good enough to argue that those views were not out of keeping with the wider social and moral context in which they were formed. The world has since changed. Canada has also moved on. The stigmata once attached to unmarried motherhood and illegitimacy are a thing of the past. Throughout the world, children conceived by artificial insemination by donor are being given the right to be told on reaching the age of majority the identity of their biological fathers. Sexual orientation is no longer stigmatised as it once was. Above all, contrary to the misgivings expressed about the inherent dangers of retrospective or retroactive law in the debate leading to the Citizenship Act, 1976, the 'Lost Canadians' legislation passed in 2008 restored or conferred rights to citizenship on that very basis.

In 2000, the Norwegian Prime Minister, Kjell Magne Bondevik, made a public apology to the *Krigsbarn*, the wartime offspring of Norwegian mothers and members of the German forces who occupied the country during the Second World War, for the discrimination they had suffered subsequently, including denial of access before 1994 to the archived files containing information about their parents' identities. Also, between 1992 and 2007, no fewer than six Prime Ministers of Japan issued public apologies for their country's treatment of the so-called 'comfort women', the women in occupied territories who were held in sexual bondage to 'service' Japanese troops. And in 2009–10, the Prime Ministers of Australia and the United Kingdom, Kevin Rudd and Gordon Brown, formally apologised to the thousands of orphaned or otherwise abandoned British children who were shipped to Australia as child migrants, some of whom could well have been the illegitimate offspring of relationships between members of Canada's armed forces and British women. Albeit belatedly and perhaps grudgingly, other governments have seen fit to apologise for the treatment meted out to those women and children. The government of Canada, on the other hand, has yet to acknowledge its war children. The silence has been deafening.

For most war children, Canadian citizenship never has been a major concern. As Joseph Taylor was advised, the avenue to citizenship through naturalisation has always been open to them. It was a path they chose not to follow. Citizenship has only loomed large in their minds because 'Fortress Canada' has deployed Canada's citizenship law as a firewall within other tightly-drawn access to information and privacy legislation. Because that legislation restricts access to public records to those with Canadian citizenship, and even then under stringent terms, war children have been denied access to the official records they would need to trace their fathers or paternal relatives.

At best, the only official assistance they have received has been from the National Archives of Canada, offering to act as an intermediary in contacting a named veteran in order to ascertain his willingness to be put in touch with the person making those enquiries. Given the strongly defensive, overtly sensitive, official stance adopted in all other aspects of Canada's treatment of its war children, it would be interesting to see the content of their communications with these veterans. Were they neutrally worded, simply stating that the sender was passing on information that an enquiry had been made? Did those letters disclose that the enquirer was a war child? In those letters or in the course of subsequent contact, were steps taken to inform the veteran recipient about his rights under the privacy and access to information legislation? The official replies that some war children received told them that their 'unanswered' letters of enquiry have been left on their (putative) fathers' files. A review of those files could be quite illuminating, for the light it would shed on their content, and the number of and outcomes of the cases involved.

Canada's evident reluctance to face up to this issue has created a theatre of both tragedy and farce. The tragedy is characterised by the persisting reluctance to provide or pay any more than a grudging lip service to those war children whose searches are unlikely to succeed without some 'inside' practical assistance. The farce is represented by cases like my own, in which the legal obstacle course has been avoided by using information from such publicly-available sources as telephone listings, obituary notices or the Royal Canadian Legion's website. It has resulted in an inherently unfair situation in which the war children who are searching for a father with an uncommon name or other readily-identifiable personal details can quite lawfully review material in the public realm, while legal restrictions block those who lack such information from accessing the official records which they need.

That unfairness, reflecting a legally-imposed inequality, has been deepened by persisting official reluctance to seek a solution that distinguishes between citizenship issues and those related to genetic inheritance. Sources like the Canadian War Brides' website confirm that citizenship may remain a pressing issue for a small minority of war brides' children, but certainly not the majority of other war children. It does not appear to have been recognised that the acquisition of Canadian citizenship has never been the driving force behind most war children's searches. If it had been, the route to citizenship through naturalisation has always been open.

In view of the disdainful treatment they have received, it could be argued that Canada's war children merit both an apology and a remedy. An apology would be a significant gesture in its own right. It would undoubtedly help to restore Canada's otherwise tarnished record. But a remedy in the form of practical measures to assist the war children's quest to 'connect' with paternal kith and kin would achieve so much more. Is it really beyond the conscience, imagination and will of the country's political, administrative and legal establishment to deliver both?

What seems to be needed is a humanitarian dispensation, derived from the principle of *jus sanguinis*, that is supportive of war children's desire to connect with paternal family (if their fathers have passed away, half-sisters and half-brothers may be more receptive to such enquiries than veterans and their wives may have been in the past), while at the same time protects privacy when it is still requested. Since that arrangement would rule out direct person-to-person communication between war children and their blood relatives, consideration should be given to the establishment within, say, the National Archives of Canada of an Office of Reconciliation charged with the task of assisting the war children with their searches.

Such proactive casework assistance could be given to both 'cold' cases from earlier years, those in which letters have been left on file, and any new enquiries that could arise in response to the greater openness that the creation of an Office of Reconciliation would foster. Quite understandably, there would be a need for appropriate safeguards. One approach might be to make access to the Office's services dependent on a formal disclaimer, obliging a prospective user to accept that any help given was provided solely on humanitarian grounds. The disclaimer should acknowledge that the assistance provided in no way whatsoever altered the user's alien status or signified any right or entitlement, either informally or within the framework of Canada's law, to initiate or pursue any claims, whether of a financial or legal nature, against either the state or its citizens, past or present. If deemed necessary, a further safeguard could restrict access to the services of an Office of Reconciliation to the war children themselves (or formally appointed representatives), thereby excluding requests for assistance from their descendants.

In today's multicultural Canada, immigrants of yesteryear retain an emotional attachment to their national roots. The Québéquois value their linguistic and cultural ties with France; Mennonites remain attached to their religious beliefs and social customs; those of West Indian descent retain a folk memory of slavery and a love of cricket; and those with Scottish forebears still celebrate their ancestral links in their pipe bands or at highland games and other gatherings. Regardless of how the legitimacy of their claim may be officially perceived, the war children are part of Canada's diaspora, with similar, if as yet unfulfilled desires to establish and celebrate their own ancestral associations, which may extend over several generations. Each and every one has an immutable inheritance. Like the lettering that runs throughout the length of a stick of seaside rock, their origins – whether Anglo-Canadian, Dutch-Canadian or other – are stamped in genetic code in every living cell. While it can be denied or dismissed as lacking legal import, that inheritance cannot be taken away. Canadians who value and celebrate their own ancestral social and cultural roots may see this, even though their law makers might still choose to turn a blind eye to its implications.

This much I have learned: the war children possess clearly-defined Canadian genetic roots which, in many instances, could be as deep as, if not deeper than, those of the members of Canada's establishment who have presumed to determine their fate. In my own case, on my father's side, my father, grandparents, four great grandparents, two great great grandparents, and three great great great grandparents were all born in Canada. The other six great great grandparents, eleven of my sixteen great great great grandparents, and six great great great great grandparents all immigrated before 1850, in most cases well before that date. With one possible exception, the abandonment of a young family by a man who could not persuade his wife to change her religious beliefs, there is nothing on record to suggest they were anything other than model citizens. Although they could lay no claim to being 'movers and shakers', they were undeniably 'salt of the earth', an essential part of the social bedrock, the foundation upon which Canada's stability, prosperity and international reputation have been built.

It is little short of scandalous, an affront to the war children, that they have been separated from their paternal roots by a combination of policies and associated law which, seemingly in the absence of any evidence beyond political tittle-tattle reinforced by a wholly unrevised legacy of Blimpish prejudice, has besmirched their mothers' reputations and provided a cover-up for their fathers by casting them as heroic young men who did no more than sow a few readily-forgiven wild oats with 'loose women'. Perpetuation of that myth should be viewed as a contravention of natural justice, which has victimised both the war children and their mothers. It is a long-standing injustice that should be remedied at the earliest opportunity. Unless a remedy is found, any claim Canada may assert to occupancy of high moral ground in the sphere of human rights, as symbolised by the establishment of the Canadian Museum of Human Rights, is bound to have an enduring hollow ring.

Bibliography

Abbott, D.C. (1946). 'Problems Related to Wives and Dependents Residing Overseas.' Report to the Cabinet Committee on Demobilization and Re-establishment, Immigration Branch. Ottawa: Department of National Defence.

Allen, Louis (1984). *Burma: The Longest War (1941–1945)*. London: J.M. Dent & Sons.

Anon. (1889). *History of the County of Middlesex, Canada*. London: The Free Press Printing Company.

Babcock, Stephen (1903). *Babcock Genealogy*. New York: Eaton & Mains.

Bell, Rev. William (1824). *Hints to Emigrants in a Series of Letters from Upper Canada*. Edinburgh: Waugh & Innes.

Borges, Jorge Luis. 'A Biography of Tadeo Isidoro Cruz (1829–1874).' In *Jorge Luis Borges: The Aleph and Other Stories*. Translated by Andrew Hurley (2000). London: Penguin Books.

Bremner, David (1869). *The Industries of Scotland: Their Rise, Progress, and Present Condition*. Edinburgh: Adam and Charles Black.

Buchanan, A.C. (1832). *Emigrants' Handbook for Arrivals in Quebec*. Quebec: Thomas Cary & Co.

Calder, Jenni (2003). *Scots in Canada*. Edinburgh: Luath Press.

Cameron, Wendy and Maude, Mary McDougall (2000). *Assisting Emigration to Upper Canada: The Petworth Project 1832–1837*. Montreal & Kingston: McGill-Queen's University Press.

Carter, Thomas (ed.) (1867). *Historical Record of the Twenty-Sixth, or Cameronian Regiment*. London: W.O. Mitchell, Military Publisher.

Clapton, Eric (2007). *Eric Clapton: The Autobiography*. London: Arrow Books.

Clements, Robert G.T. and Clements, Sheila (2004). *The Clements Family*. Ontario: Authors.

Cobbett, William (1830). *Rural Rides*. Republished in 1967. London: Penguin Books.

Cole, J.R. (1889). *History of Washington and Kent Counties, Rhode Island*. New York: W.W. Preston & Co.

Cooper, J. Fenimore (1826). *The Last of the Mohicans*. Republished in 1954. London: Collins Library of Classics.

Copp, Terry (2006). *Cinderella Army: The Canadians in Northwest Europe 1944–1945*. Toronto: University of Toronto Press.

Costello, John (1984). *Love, Sex and War: Changing Values, 1939–45*. London: Guild Publishing.

Craig, David (1990). *On the Crofters' Trail: In Search of the Clearance Highlanders*. London: Jonathan Cape.

Crittall, Elizabeth (ed.), (1965). 'Corsley.' *Victoria County History: A History of the County of Wiltshire*. Vol. 8, 13–25. London: Oxford University Press for the University of London Institute of Historical Research.

Denison, Rev. Frederic (1878). *Westerly (Rhode Island) and its Witnesses 1626–1876*. Providence RI: J.A. & R.A. Reid.

Devine, T.M. (2004). *Scotland's Empire 1600–1815*. London: Penguin Books.

Ellis, Col G. (1947). *History of the Directorate of Repatriation and Servicemen's Dependents*. Ottawa: Department of National Defence.

Franklin, William (2005). *Burwell: The History of a Fen-edge Village*. King's Lynn: Heritage Marketing & Publications.

Graves, Robert (1929). *Goodbye to All That*. London: Jonathan Cape.

Grayze, Susan R. (1997). Mothers, Marraines, and Prostitutes: Morale and Morality in First World War France. *The International History Review,* **19** (1), 66–82.

Greer, Germaine (1970). *The Female Eunuch*. London: MacGibbon & Key.

Gregg, Pauline (1965). *A Social and Economic History of Britain 1760–1965*. Fifth Edition. London: George G. Harrap & Co.

Hadley, C. (undated). *Cambridge History: A Personal View*. At: http://www.cl.cam.ac.uk/

Hammond, J.L. and Hammond, Barbara (1911). *The Village Labourer 1760–1832: A Study in the Government of England before the Reform Bill*. London: Longman Green & Co.

Harrison, J.F.C. (1984). *The Common People: A History from the Norman Conquest to the Present*. London: Fontana.

Haste, Cate (1992). *Rules of Desire: Sex in Britain, World War I to the Present*. London: Chatto & Windus.

Herrington, Walter S. (1913). *History of the County of Lennox and Addington*. Toronto: Macmillan.

Howells, Gary (2003). ' "On Account of their Disreputable Characters": Parish-Assisted Emigration from Rural England, 1834–1860.' *History*, **88** (292), 587–605.

Humphreys, Margaret (1995). *Empty Cradles*. London: Corgi Books.

Hurdle, Bessie (1973). *The History of Newbury*. Newbury ON: The Bothwell Times.

Keshen, Jeffrey A. (2004). *Saints, Sinners, and Soldiers: Canada's Second World War*. Vancouver: University of British Columbia Press.

Jarratt, Melynda (2007). *War Brides: The stories of the women who left everything behind to follow the men they loved*. Stroud: Tempus Publishing.

Jasanoff, Maya (2011). *Liberty's Exiles: The Loss of America and the Remaking of the British Empire*. London: Harper Press.

Johnston, Marion (ed.), (1974). *The Family Tree of the Armstrongs of Newbury*. Petrolia: Petrolia Print & Litho Ltd.

Lawrie, Alex C. (1980). *Dalkeith Through the Ages*. Dalkeith: T. Kemp.

Mandell, Daniel R. (2010). *King Philip's War: Colonial Expansion, Native Resistance and the End of Indian Sovereignty*. Baltimore: The John Hopkins University Press.

McGill University (2001). In Search of Your Canadian Past: The Canada County Atlas Digital Project. At: http://digital.library.mcgill.ca/

Moir, David Macbeth (1828). *The Life of Mansie Wauch: Tailor in Dalkeith*. Edinbugh: W. Blackwood.

Moodie, Susanna (1857). *Roughing it in the Bush; or Life in Canada*. London: Richard Bentley.

Occomore, David (ed.), (2005). *The Burwell Chronicle: A Century of Life in a Cambridgeshire Village*. Bury St Edmunds: Burwell History Society & St Edmundsbury Press.

Philbrick, Nathaniel (2007). *Mayflower: A Voyage to War*. London: Harper Perennial.

Pipher, Mary (1995). *Reviving Ophelia*. New York: Ballantine Books.

Plimpton, Ruth Talbot (1994). *Mary Dyer: Biography of a Quaker Rebel*. Boston: Branden Publishing Co.

Poulett Scrope, G. (1832). *Extracts of Letters from Poor Persons who Emigrated Last Year to Canada and the United States*. Second Edition. London: James Ridgway.

Radune, Richard (2005). *Pequot Plantation: The Story of an Early Colonial Settlement.* Branford CT: Research in Time Publications.

Rains, Olga; Rains, Lloyd, and Jarratt, Melynda (2006). *Voices of the Left Behind: Project Roots and the Canadian War Children of World War II.* Toronto: Dundurn Press.

Richardson, Heather (1990). *Burwell: A Stroll through History.* Cambridge: H.M. Richardson Publishing.

Robinson, Caroline E. (1895). *The Hazard family of Rhode Island 1635–1894.* Boston: Author.

Ross, Andrew (1918). 'The Cameronians (Scottish Rifles): 1. The 26th Cameronian Regiment.' In: Sir Herbert Maxwell (ed.). *The Lowland Scots Regiments: Their Origins, Character and Services Previous to the Great War of 1914.* Glasgow: James Maclehose & Sons.

See, Scott W. (2001). *The History of Canada.* Westport CT: Greenwood Press.

Smith, David R. (1985). 'The Ironmill.' *Old Dalkeith,* **2**, 7–8. Dalkeith: Dalkeith History Society.

Smith, William H. (1846). *Smith's Canadian Gazetteer; Comprising Statistical and General Information Respecting All Parts of the Upper Province, or Canada West.* Toronto: H. & W. Rowsell.

Smout, T. C. (ed.), (1978). 'Journal of Henry Kalmeter's Travels in Scotland.' In: *Scottish Industrial History: A Miscellany.* Edinburgh: T. & C. Constable for The Scottish History Society.

Sokoloff, Sally (1999). ' "How are they at home?": Community, state and servicemen's wives in England, 1939–45.' *Women's History Review,* **8**: 1, 27–52.

Stacey, C.P. (1944). *Canadian Relations with the People of the United Kingdom and the General Problem of Morale.* Directorate of History and Heritage CMHQ Report 119. Ottawa: Department of National Defence.

Stacey, C.P. (1955). *Official History of the Canadian Army in the Second World War, Vol. I: Six Years of War: The Army in Canada, Britain and the Pacific.* Ottawa: The Queen's Printer.

Stacey, C.P. (1960). *Official History of the Canadian Army in the Second World War, Vol. III: The Victory Campaign; The Operations in North-West Europe 1944–1945.* Ottawa: The Queen's Printer.

Stacey, C.P. and Wilson, Barbara M. (1987). *The Half-Million: The Canadians in Britain, 1939–1946.* Toronto: University of Toronto Press.

United Nations (1966). *International Covenant on Civil and Political Rights.* New York: United Nations.

United Nations (1989). *Convention on the Rights of the Child.* New York: United Nations.

Vance, Michael E. (1992). 'The Politics of Emigration: Scotland and Assisted Emigration to Upper Canada, 1815–26.' In: T.M. Devine (ed.). *Scottish Emigration and Scottish Society,* 37–60. Edinburgh: John Donald Publishers Ltd.

Wareham, A.F. and Wright, A.P.M. (eds.), (2002). 'Burwell.' *The Victoria History of the County of Cambridge and the Isle of Ely.* Vol. 10, 334–369. London: Oxford University Press for the University of London Institute of Historical Research.

Warner Collection (undated). *The Simpson Letters.* http://zonzorp.ca/tedd/simpson_warner/

Wheatley, Dennis (1978). *The Time Has Come: Officer and Temporary Gentleman 1914–1919.* London: Hutchinson.

Wood, David J. (2000). *Making Ontario: Agricultural Colonization and Landscape Re-creation before the Railway.* Montreal & Kingston: McGill-Queen's University Press.

Acknowledgements

This book, the story it has to tell and the research on which it is based, would simply not have been feasible without the Internet and the access which it has provided to so many different sources. Certainly, the family history it records would not have been possible without the information gained through my worldwide membership of Ancestry.co.uk and access to other family history websites. And the interpretation of that information would have been much less fully-informed but for Internet access to geographically-distant websites and out of print publications, now accessible through Google and similar open sources.

But, as any seasoned 'surfer' will readily recognise, it is virtually impossible to keep track of each and every website visited, particularly when one is hot on the scent of a potentially promising new line of enquiry. For that reason, I can only apologise for any unintentional omission from the list.

In addition to Ancestry.co.uk, special mention should be made to the Canadian War Brides website, the repository of, or pointer to, much of the archived official documentation to which reference is made in the Afterword. Other Internet-based sources on which I have relied include the following: BMD (UK birth, marriage and death records); British History Online; Cambridgeshire Family History Society; Citizenship and Immigration Canada; Cyndi's List; Department of National Defence, Canada (Directorate of History and Heritage); Genes Reunited; Global Genealogy; Granny's Genealogy Garden; In Search of Your Canadian Past (Canadian County Atlas Digital Project, McGill University); International Genealogical

Index; Lanark County Genealogical Society; Lost Canadians; Multicultural Canada; Ontario Cemetery Finding Aid; Ontario Genealogical Society (Elgin, Lambton, London and Middlesex, and Perth County branches); Ontario Heritage Trust; Rootsweb.com; Royal Canadian Legion; Scotland's People; Statistics Canada; Upper Canada Genealogy; and Veterans Affairs Canada.

Research also involved visits to the Family History Centre, Church of Jesus Christ of the Latter-day Saints, Morningside, Edinburgh; Glencoe and District Historical Society, Southwest Middlesex; the Lambton Room, Wyoming, Lambton County; the Local Studies and Archive Service, Loanhead, Midlothian; the Public Record Office for Northern Ireland, Belfast; and Register House, Edinburgh. The courteous and helpful responses to my enquiries in all of those locations were much appreciated. In similar vein, I wish to record my indebtedness to Penny Samek of Heritage Investigations, Lanark, Ontario for commissioned research that led to the unearthing of some ancestral land holding and military records, and Leonard Bowyer of Burwell History Society for sharing his work on the village tithe map and associated records.

There is also the wholly unredeemable debt I now owe members of my newly-found Canadian family. They not only provided the warmest of welcomes to their midst but also, in a most generous sharing of memories, mementos, family records and photographs, added colour and texture to the lives of my late father and his forebears that could never have been gleaned from more impersonal, formal or official sources. In that context, the principal informants have been my sister, Marlene Newby, and my aunt, my father's youngest sister, Shirley Ann Muni, both of whom have taken considerable time and trouble to ensure that I received the fullest imaginable 'warts and all' account of my father's life and family background. Others who have added significantly to that picture include my father's first cousins Joseph Babcock, Kathleen Clements and the late Philip Clements.

The paternal family tree reproduced in the text is published in accordance with the Ancestry.co.uk terms and conditions for limited use licence for data that are part of a unique family history (16 February 2011). The opportunity to make such use of my personal family history data, for the accuracy of which I am solely responsible, is appreciated. For her generous permission to make extensive use of the Warner Collection of letters written by members of the Simpson family, I wish also to thank Thelma Warner, the current custodian of that privately-held correspondence.

Melynda Jarratt, Gillian McGovern, Douglas McKenzie and Herbert Williams have read earlier drafts either as extracts or in full. I am most obliged for their comments and suggestions. The professional attention and practical assistance provided by Carol Biss and her colleagues at Book Guild Publishing – Joanna Bentley, Managing Editor; Janet Wrench and Victoria Regan, who have overseen production; Imogen Palmer and Christina Harkness, who undertook the copy-editing and proof reading; and Kieran Hood, who contributed his design talents – has been most impressive, and is also gratefully acknowledged.

Last, but certainly not least, I must record a very special debt of gratitude to my wife, Fay, to whom this work is dedicated. Undoubtedly, the at times obsessive pursuit of my family history research and the extensive follow-up to those enquiries tried her patience to the limit. But she was supportive throughout and the book has benefited greatly from her incisive appraisal of its progress at every stage. Yet more significantly, whenever needed, she was always on hand to provide sympathetic support and encouragement. In short, I could not have wished for a better travelling companion with whom to share the long journey to what has become our personal 'new world'.